LRC

# RETRIEVER

## AN OWNER'S GUIDE

# The authors

**Valerie Foss** is a well-known judge, author and columnist. She has judged six times at Crufts, including Golden and Flat Coated Retrievers, as well as the Gundog Group in 1995 where her winner went on to Best in Show. She writes a weekly breed note column in the British canine newspaper *Dog World*, and her Elswood prefix is internationally renowned. She has bred and owned top class English Setters and Golden Retrievers, including fifteen Show Champions.

**John Bower BVSc, MRCVS** is a senior partner in a small animal Veterinary Hospital in Plymouth, England. He has served as President of both the British Veterinary Association and the British Small Animal Veterinary Association. He writes regularly for the veterinary press and also for dog and cat publications. He is co-author of two dog healthcare books and a member of the Kennel Club.

**Caroline Bower BVM&S, MRCVS** runs a veterinary health centre in the same practice as John. Her special interests include prevention and treatment of behavioural problems, and she lectures to dog breeding and training groups.

COLLINS

# RETRIEVER

## AN OWNER'S GUIDE

## Valerie Foss

HarperCollins*Publishers*

First published in 1997 by
HarperCollins*Publishers*
London

A catalogue record of this book is available
from the British Library

ISBN 0 00 412970 9

This book was created by SP Creative Design for HarperCollins*Publishers* Ltd
Editor: Heather Thomas
Designer: Al Rockall and Rolando Ugolini
Production: Rolando Ugolini
Illustrations: Al Rockall and Rolando Ugolini

**Photography:**
François Nicaise: pages 1, 3, 6-7, 9, 10, 11, 12, 13, 21, 23, 26, 29, 31, 34, 36, 44-45, 47, 49, 50, 55, 56, 59, 61, 62, 64, 65, 67, 69, 72, 75, 76, 79, 81, 83, 85, 87, 93, 94-95
David Dalton: pages 14-15, 16-17, 18-19, 24, 27, 28, 30, 32, 35, 37, 38, 39, 40, 41, 42, 43, 52, 54, 57, 58, 88, 91

**Acknowledgements**
The publishers would like to thank the following for their kind assistance in producing this book: Scampers School for Dogs for their help with photography, and special thanks to Charlie Clarricoates for all his hard work, Pat Tuck and her Golden Retrievers Captain (Tamsbrook Trouble at Sea) and Jenny (Hodenhoe Happiness is with Tambrook), Ann Taggart and her Golden Retrievers Hunter (Altindan Guitar Man) and Dorcas (Rosgar Luck be a Lady of Altindan), Angela Clark and Hannah (Alibren Jean Genie of Redtowers), Deborah Miller and her Flat-coated Retriever Poppy (Millreed Water Nymph), Sarah Whittaker and Dana (Bramatha Northern Dancer), Rio and Coco (Stonemead Chocolate Drop), Mr and Mrs David Knott and Millie (Bramatha Coffee Capri) Brenda Mellars and Leo (Cwmgilli Wildfowler).

Colour reproduction by Colourscan, Singapore
Printed and bound by New Interlitho SpA, Italy

# CONTENTS

## PART ONE – YOU AND YOUR DOG

## PART TWO – CARING FOR YOUR DOG

## PART THREE – HEALTHCARE

# YOU AND YOUR DOG

Retrievers are among the most popular and well-loved dogs. Their temperament, kindly nature and intelligence make them ideal family pets and companions as well as hard-working gundogs. They are natural retrievers and love to carry things, whether it's game birds, toys or your new shoes. Like other intelligent dogs, they need plenty of exercise and mental stimulation, and Retriever owners must be prepared to spend a great deal of time with their dogs. However, the joys of owning one of these lovely dogs bring their own rewards. Golden Retrievers are also used as Guide Dogs for the Blind, Hearing Dogs for the Deaf and PAT dogs.

# EARLY HISTORY

Featured in this book are three Retrievers: the Golden Retriever, the Flat Coated Retriever and the Curly Coated Retriever. The Golden and Flat Coat share a common ancestor – the Wavy Coated Retriever – and we will examine these two breeds first. Unlike Spaniels and Setters, which were mentioned as far back as the fourteenth century, the Retrievers are relatively recent breeds in the canine world. Only from 1830 onwards are they recorded; this was when sportsmen started to develop a breed to use specifically for retrieving shot game.

## Gundogs

In the eighteenth and nineteenth centuries, shooting was part of country life, and the dogs most commonly used were Setters and Pointers. They found the game and then waited whilst it was shot. By the beginning of the nineteenth century, sportsmen were beginning to train their Setters and Pointers to retrieve in addition to putting up the birds, but this had a tendency to spoil their setter work. Therefore the need was recognised for a working dog bred solely

for retrieving. At this stage, as the objective was to pass on working ability, the gundog breeds were mated amongst themselves. The retrieving Setters were crossed with the small St John's Newfoundland, which had been brought to the British Isles by the Newfoundland fishing fleets when they unloaded their catches in ports in southern and north-eastern England.

## The Wavy Coated Retriever

The result of this cross-breeding was a heavy, wavy-coated dog, which was known as the Wavy Coated Retriever (the name 'flat coat' is used much later). With a shortish skull, it was a heavy-boned dog, tan and brindle in colour – more evidence of its setter base. Next a dash of Scotch Collie was introduced, eliminating the wavy coat and feathering of the setter.

The man who would have the greatest influence on developing the Flat Coat Retriever was S.E. Shirley. From his large

*The Golden Retriever evolved from matings between Wavy Coated Retrievers and Tweed Water Spaniels in the mid-nineteenth century.*

kennels, he fixed the type of the Flat Coated Retriever. He is also notable for founding the Kennel Club in 1873, and he became its first chairman and President.

## The Golden Retriever

The most influential early breeder of the Golden Retriever was Dudley Coutts Majoribanks, the first Lord Tweedmouth. The first breeding took place at his holiday estate, Guisachen, near Inverness in the Scottish Highlands. Whilst in Brighton in the 1860s, he saw and bought a good looking young yellow Retriever, originally from a gamekeeper on Lord Chichester's estate at nearby Stanmer. This dog was the only yellow puppy out of a black wavy-coated litter.

*Flat Coated Retrievers are less well known than the ubiquitous Golden Retriever.*

This phenomenon seemed to happen quite often, possibly because of the mixed bloodlines behind the black Retrievers.

Dr Bond Moore, who had a famous Retriever kennel in the mid-nineteenth century, is recorded as having a litter of Ch. Midnights (black) which included two fine pups of a pale liver colour. There were many of these pups in otherwise all black litters, and what we recognise today as 'liver' does not cover the colour variations mentioned in those days, which included a wide range of sandy colours, from yellows to browns.

Lord Tweedmouth called his new dog

Nous (the Gaelic word for wisdom), and the dog is mentioned in the kennel records as Lord Chichester's breed, pupped June 1864. Nous was mated in 1868 to a Tweed Water Spaniel called Belle (these dogs are now extinct but they were the shape and size of a Retriever and came in various colours, including liver). In Nous and Belle's first litter were Crocus, Cowslip and Primrose, and a later litter produced Ada. These puppies were the root foundation of Golden Retrievers as a distinct breed.

## Curly Coated Retrievers

The origin of the Curly has caused much speculation. The available evidence tends to make this dog the longest established of the three retriever breeds. The Curly has a coat whose texture and curls are unique, and this could have been inherited from the curled water dog. Its ancestors include the Irish Water Spaniel and the Llanidloes Welsh Setter. By the early nineteenth century, the Curly had evolved in its present form. Up until 1864, all the retriever varieties were shown together; they later split into the Curly Coated, Flat Coated and Golden Retrievers, as we know them today.

*The Curly Coated Retriever may claim the longest established history of all the Retrievers.*

# 2

# BREED STANDARDS

## WHAT IS A STANDARD?

What is a standard? It is the perfect description of a breed of dog against which we measure the dog in order to see that, as much as possible, it conforms to the written description. The Breed Standards belong to the Kennel Club, which has a special Breed Standards and Stud Book committee, with representatives from all the groups:

Gundogs, Hounds, Terriers, Utility, Working and Toy dogs. The wording in the Standard can be changed only by the committee, and there must be sound

*This is a good example of a balanced dog with no exaggerations. Breeders strive to produce a dog that conforms to the Breed Standard.*

*This gundog is waiting patiently to do the job for which the breed was evolved.*

reasons for doing so. Thus it cannot be changed in order to fit in with the dogs being shown at any given time.

The Retrievers are included in the Gundog group. In the early days of these three breeds, the influential breeders and the first breed clubs developed the first written standards. The Curly Coated Retriever Club was established in 1890, The Golden Retriever Club in 1911, and The Flat Coated Retriever Association in 1923. All the Standards have been written for a working gundog, and this is why any exaggerations cannot be allowed.

# GOLDEN RETRIEVER — BREED STANDARD

Reproduced by kind permission of the Kennel Club

**General Appearance** Symmetrical, balanced, active, powerful, level mover; sound with kindly expression.

**Characteristics** Biddable, intelligent and possessing natural working ability.

**Temperament** Kindly, friendly and confident.

**Colour** Any shade of gold or cream, neither red nor mahogany. A few white hairs on chest only, permissible.

**Size** Height at withers: dogs: 56-61 cms (22-24 ins); bitches: 51-56 cms (20-22 ins).

**Faults** Any departure from the foregoing points should be considered a fault and the seriousness with which the fault should be regarded should be in exact proportion to its degree.

**Note** Male animals should have two apparently normal testicles fully descended into the scrotum.

**Tail** Set on and carried level with back, reaching to hocks, without curl at tip.

**Body** Balanced, short-coupled, deep through heart. Ribs deep, well sprung. Level topline.

**Hindquarters** Loin and legs strong and muscular, good second thighs, well bent stifles. Hocks well let down, straight when viewed from rear, neither turning in nor out. Cow-hocks highly undesirable.

**Gait/Movement** Powerful with good drive. Straight and true in front and rear. Stride long and free with no sign of hackney action in front.

**Feet** Round and cat-like.

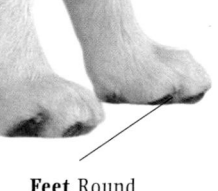

**Head and Skull** Balanced and well chiselled, skull broad without coarseness; well set on neck, muzzle powerful, wide and deep. Length of foreface approximately equals length from well defined stop to occiput. Nose preferably black.

**Eyes** Dark brown, set well apart, dark rims.

**Ears** Moderate size, set on approximate level with eyes.

**Neck** Good length, clean and muscular.

**Mouth** Jaws strong, with a perfect, regular and complete scissor bite, i.e. upper teeth closely overlapping lower teeth and set square to the jaws.

### COAT

Flat or wavy with good feathering, dense water-resisting undercoat.

**Forequarters** Forelegs straight with good bone, shoulders well laid back, long in blade with upper arm of equal length placing legs well under body. Elbows close fitting.

## FLAT COATED RETRIEVER – BREED STANDARD

Reproduced by kind permission of the Kennel Club

**General Appearance** A bright, active dog of medium size with an intelligent expression, showing power without lumber, and raciness without weediness.

**Characteristics** Generously endowed with natural gundog ability, optimism and friendliness demonstrated by enthusiastic tail action.

**Temperament** Confident & kindly.

**Colour** Black or liver only.

**Size** Preferred height:
dogs: 58-61 cms (23-24 ins); bitches: 56-59 cms (22-23 ins).
Preferred weight in hard condition: dogs: 25-35 kgs (60-80 lbs); bitches: 25-34 kgs (55-70 lbs).

**Faults** Any departure from the foregoing points should be considered a fault and the seriousness with which the fault should be regarded should be in exact proportion to its degree.

**Note** Male animals should have two apparently normal testicles fully descended into the scrotum.

**Tail** Short, straight and well set on, gaily carried, but never much above level of back.

**Body** Foreribs fairly flat. Body, well ribbed up showing a gradual spring and well arched in centre but rather lighter towards quarters. Loin short and square. Open couplings highly undesirable.

**Hindquarters** Muscular. Moderate bend of stifle and hock, latter well let down. Should stand true all round. Cowhocks highly undesirable.

16

**Head and Skull** Head, long and nicely moulded. Skull, flat and moderately broad with a slight stop between eyes, in no way accentuated, avoiding a down or dish-faced appearance. Nose of good size, with open nostrils. Jaws long and strong, capable of carrying a hare or pheasant.

**Ears** Small and well set on, close to side of head.

**Eyes** Medium size, dark brown or hazel, with a very intelligent expression (a round prominent eye highly undesirable). Not obliquely placed.

**Mouth** Jaws strong with a perfect, regular and complete scissor bite, i.e. upper teeth closely overlapping lower teeth and set square to the jaws. Teeth sound and strong.

**Neck** Head well set in neck, the latter reasonably long and free from throatiness, symmetrically set and obliquely placed in shoulders, running well into the back to allow for easy seeking of trail.

**Forequarters** Chest deep and fairly broad, with well defined brisket, on which elbows should move cleanly and evenly. Forelegs straight, with bone of good quality throughout.

## COAT

Dense, of fine to medium texture and good quality, as flat as possible. Legs and tail well feathered. Full furnishings on maturity complete the elegance of a good dog.

**Gait/Movement** Free and flowing, straight and true as seen from front and rear.

**Feet** Round and strong with toes close and well arched. Soles thick and strong.

# CURLY COATED RETRIEVER – BREED STANDARD

Reproduced by kind permission of the Kennel Club

**General Appearance** Strong, active, smart, upstanding, with distinctive coat.

**Characteristics** Intelligent with endurance.

**Temperament** Friendly and confident.

**Colour** Black or liver.

**Size** Desirable height at withers: dogs: 68.58 cms (27 ins); bitches: 63.5 cms (25 ins).

**Faults** Any departure from the foregoing points should be considered a fault and the seriousness with which the fault should be regarded should be in exact proportion to its degree.

**Note** Male animals should have two apparently normal testicles fully descended into the scrotum.

**Tail** Moderately short, carried straight, covered with curls, tapering towards point, never gay or curled.

**Body** Well sprung ribs, good depth of brisket, not long in loin or tucked-up.

**Hindquarters** Strong, muscular, hock low to ground and well bent.

**Feet** Round, compact, toes well arched.

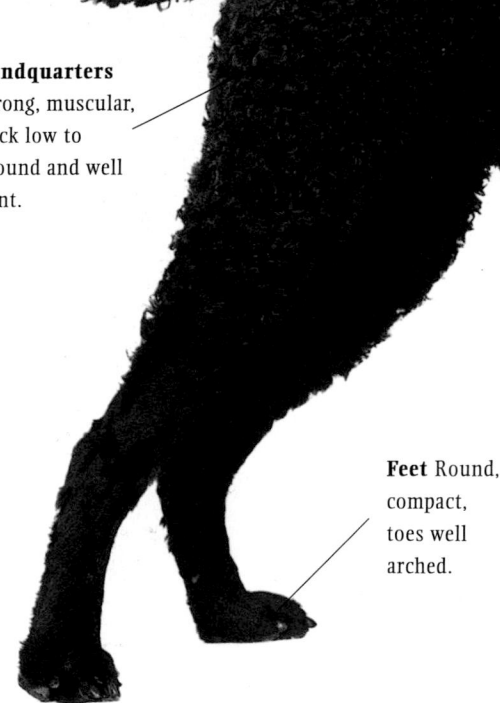

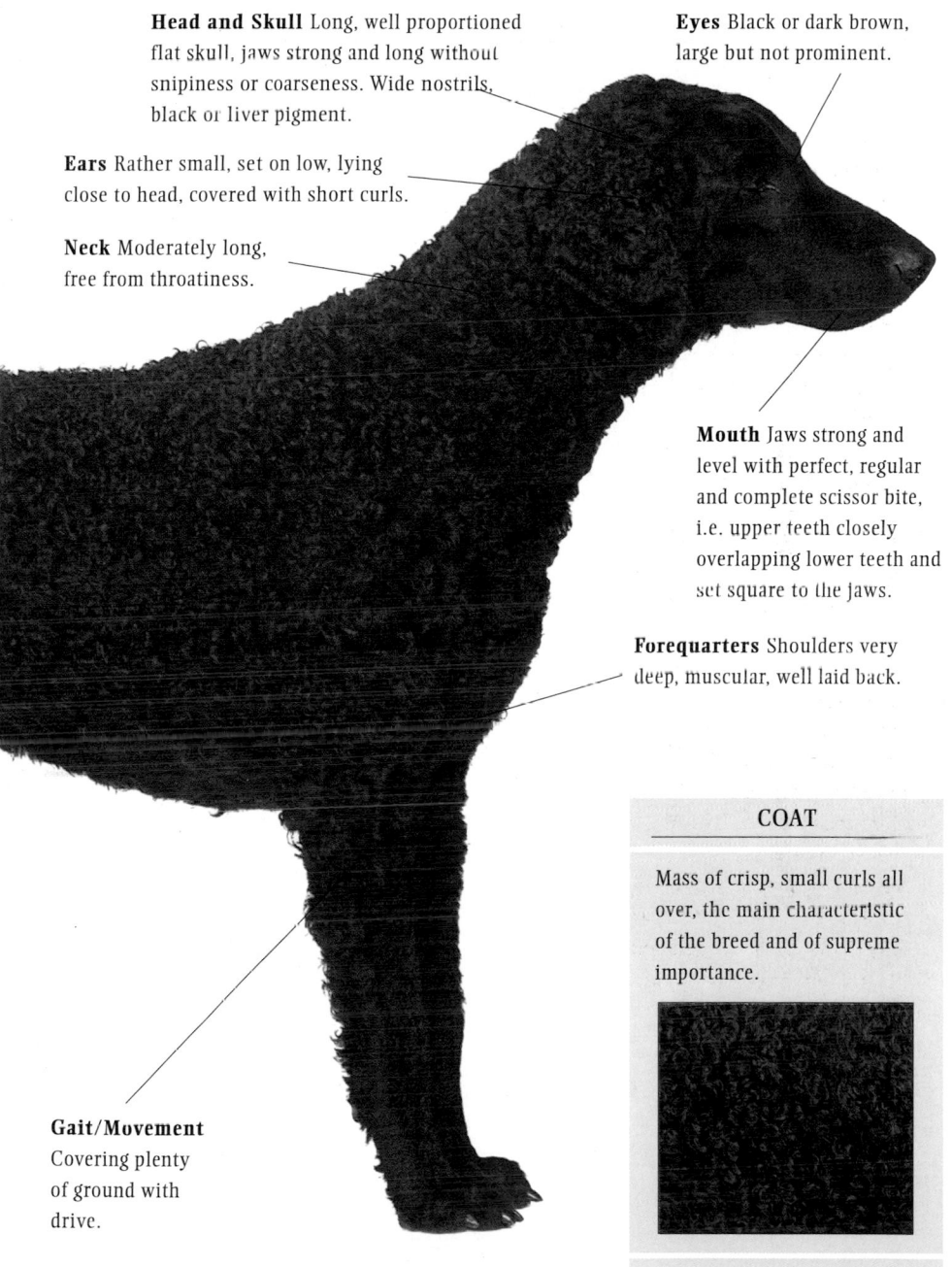

**Head and Skull** Long, well proportioned flat skull, jaws strong and long without snipiness or coarseness. Wide nostrils, black or liver pigment.

**Ears** Rather small, set on low, lying close to head, covered with short curls.

**Neck** Moderately long, free from throatiness.

**Eyes** Black or dark brown, large but not prominent.

**Mouth** Jaws strong and level with perfect, regular and complete scissor bite, i.e. upper teeth closely overlapping lower teeth and set square to the jaws.

**Forequarters** Shoulders very deep, muscular, well laid back.

**Gait/Movement** Covering plenty of ground with drive.

## COAT

Mass of crisp, small curls all over, the main characteristic of the breed and of supreme importance.

## THE STANDARDS IN DEPTH

Now let's look at the standards more closely; they all follow the same format under the same headings.

■ **The General Appearance** describes the general shape and outlook of each breed. All Retrievers should be balanced, kindly and intelligent; and the curly general appearance tells us straight away about their most distinctive feature – their coat.

■ **The Characteristics and Temperament** confirm that all the Retrievers are friendly. The job they were initially formed and bred to do was to be a gundog, working happily amongst other dogs – not to be a watchdog or guard-dog. One should never try to turn the temperament of one breed into that of another, and it is important to buy the right dog for the right job.

■ **The Head** really shows you whether the dog is typical of its breed. The mouth is the same for all three Retrievers: a regular and perfect scissor bite, i.e. the upper teeth closely overlapping the lower teeth and set square to the jaws.

■ **The Neck and Shoulders** must be reasonably long and with a good lay back of the shoulders as all three Retrievers must be able to follow a ground scent easily.

■ **The Body** of each breed should be short coupled, balanced deep, with a good spring of the ribs and not flat. Again, when working all three Retrievers need plenty of lung room for expansion, and strong quarters in order to work all day.

■ **The Feet** should be round as all three Retrievers work on the same type of terrain (not like the Saluki, for example, which is a desert dog), and they are all good in water and strong swimmers.

■ **Their Coats** should be dense, but the Curly Coated Retriever should have a mass of crisp small curls all over. This is the principal characteristic of the breed and is of supreme importance.

■ **In Colour** the Golden Retriever can be any shade of gold or cream, but red or mahogany are not permissible, and it can have only a few white hairs on the chest. One important point to remember is that there isn't a correct colour! Any shade of gold or cream is permitted, and that gives you quite a variation. People who speak of the correct colour are usually referring to the shade they happen to prefer themselves or the colour of their dog. Flat Coats and Curly Coats come in black or liver.

■ **The Size** depends on the breed of Retriever. The dog's height is measured at the withers where the neck joins the body.

■ **The Note** at the end of each Standard is the same, i.e. that male animals should have two apparently normal testicles fully descended into the scrotum. If, for health reasons, your dog has been castrated, then you should contact the Kennel Club to find out whether they will allow you to show your dog. A certificate from your vet will be necessary.

## Other Retrievers

The Chesapeake Bay Retriever (above) took its name from the cold waters of that North American bay where it was used for retrieving. An active worker with a distinctive harsh, oily outer coat and a dense, woolly undercoat, it works in adverse weather conditions, including ice and snow. Chesapeakes are independent, intelligent, affectionate and courageous with a great love of water. They make good guardians and companions.

The Nova Scotia Duck Tolling Retriever (right) was originally used to lure waterfowl into a decoy. A strong swimmer, it is kind, confident and easy to train. However, like the Chesapeake Bay Retriever, they are still very rare in

Britain and in 1995 only fifty-nine dogs were registered with the Kennel Club.

3

# BEHAVIOUR AND TRAINING

## EARLY TRAINING

Your dog has to be trained to become socially acceptable and to fit into your family life. Owning a dog is a responsibility, but it is one that adds a lot to your enjoyment. Just as the summers of our childhood always seem bathed in a rosy glow and it never rained, so the dogs owned by our parents seemed to train themselves, exercise themselves and be fed perfectly adequately on household scraps! This was probably because we never investigated the hard work and responsibility involved in owning a dog.

Also, many people tend to assume that dogs are very economical to keep and cost little to feed and maintain. However, to buy a well bred, well reared puppy who will grow up into a good representative of the breed you have chosen, will not be cheap, and will also involve you in a great deal of work and time in training him.

### Chewing

All puppies have to be house-trained; you must endure the teething stage when they can chew literally anything and everything. Puppies need to chew,

especially between four and six months of age, when their milk teeth are being replaced by adult teeth. During this time, you should make sure that if your puppy is left alone, he cannot chew potentially dangerous items, such as electric wires, cables and plugs. Nor should you give him old shoes to cut his teeth on. The puppy does not know the difference between old and new, and could ruin your best shoes at a later date – he will not understand why you are so annoyed with him.

■ You can buy special chew toys from your local pet shop, or your butcher may let you have some large marrow bones. However, these can only be used for a couple of days and then must be thrown away. You can purchase smoked or sterilized bones from most pet shops, which last for a long time.

■ If you have an older dog already, put the puppy in his playpen or crate when it's bone eating time so that he does not try to rob the older dog of his bone and cause trouble.

■ If you find that your puppy is chewing something forbidden, gently take it out of his mouth, saying 'No' in a firm voice.

## Verbal commands

Whenever the command 'No' is used, remember that your voice has also to show your displeasure so it must be a different tone from your usual speaking voice. Always keep your dog vocabulary simple and stick to basic commands such as: 'No', 'Good dog', 'Stay' and 'Come'.

## Behaviour problems

Many people have behavioural problems which can be sorted out, and dogs are not so very different. Nowadays, there is a

*It is always a good idea to keep vocabulary simple when training a dog. All the members of the family should use the same commands to avoid confusion.*

general awareness that most animal behavioural problems can be avoided, particularly through the adequate socialization of puppies. However, if an adult dog does have problems, then it is possible to consult an expert, such as a pet behaviour counsellor.

## Socialization

Socialization of puppies means that they learn to relate to people and to other dogs. The puppy must become accustomed to a range of different environments and experiences, and this is called habituation. Scientific research has shown that the important socialization and habituation period for a puppy is up to twelve to fourteen weeks of age.

As puppies remain with the breeder until they are at least seven weeks old, the breeder should do as much socialization as possible before they go to their new homes. When the puppy comes to you, it's your turn to take over. However, new owners hit a problem straight away: the vaccination programme.

24

## THE VACCINATION PROGRAMME

This programme is essential for the puppy's health and wellbeing, but it does mean that he must be kept away from sources of infection until the programme is complete, usually after twelve weeks of age. Therefore the puppy cannot venture out of your house and garden during the named period. The vaccination programme works as follows:

**1** It starts when the bitch has her litter, and she passes on antibodies (immunity) to infectious diseases through her milk to her puppies.

**2** The level of the immunity gradually decreases so that by twelve weeks most puppies have lost their effective immunity to infection. The level of immunity diminishes at different rates from one puppy to another. This is why it is usually recommended that the vaccination programme should be started at twelve weeks. It can be started at an earlier age if your vet agrees, and this is something that you may wish to discuss with him.

## The process of socialization

■ From five to seven weeks old, the puppies learn about canine socialization with their littermates, and their mother, as pack leader, teaches them further behaviour.

■ From the eighth to the twelfth weeks, socialization continues with humans. This process starts when the puppy leaves the litter and moves away from the mother's influence.

■ From the thirteenth to the sixteenth week is the time for building up security and love, as the puppy grows in size in his new environment. As he becomes more familiar with his new home, his confidence will grow. If the household contains young children, it is important that you supervise gentle play, for the sake of both the puppy and the children. Even small children can be quite rough, and the most gentle pup can give a child a playful nip or may be pushed beyond endurance by constant teasing.

■ From this age, gentle discipline should be introduced. The word 'No' said in the firmer tone of voice really starts to mean something, and the puppy should respond to it.

## Getting used to a name

From the moment you pick your puppy up and bring him home, you should use the name you have chosen for him as

### ANNUAL BOOSTERS

One thing to remember is that an annual booster injection is required for the rest of your dog's life, and your vet will send you a card to remind you when it is due.

much as possible. When he responds and comes to you, reward him with lots of praise and love before allowing him to wander off.

Sit out in the garden, calling the puppy to you, and sometimes give him a small titbit when he comes to you very quickly. This reinforces in his mind the association of name, response and praise, and sometimes food from his leader.

## Meeting people

Before the vaccination programme is completed, take the puppy out in the car, and get him used to car travel. Visit

*Playtime for a puppy with his litter-mates is also important in the process of learning and socialization.*

friends or relations, carrying your puppy. He should be encouraged to meet as many people as possible of all ages. However, ensure that the houses you visit do not have dogs at this vulnerable stage in his vaccination programme.

From the beginning, accustom your puppy to lots of visitors. Let them play with him, but don't allow the puppy to get too rough. If this happens, stop him, gently but firmly.

## Noise and cats

Do not allow the puppy to climb on the furniture. If he does this, make him get back down onto the floor, saying 'No' in your special firm tone of voice, and then divert his attention.

From the beginning, get your puppy used to all the domestic noises in the house, such as the vacuum cleaner, washing machine and television. He should also become accustomed to the lawn mower but watch the electric cable if you have an electric model. Build up the noise level gradually – not too much at first while he is still quite timid and may be easily frightened.

If you have a cat, it is important that it lives in harmony with your puppy. So introduce the puppy in a controlled environment. Most cats tend to keep well out of a puppy's way and soon learn not to run away from their own family dog – if they don't run, the dog usually doesn't chase.

## Home alone

From the beginning you must train your puppy to be left alone for short periods. Puppies who are not accustomed to being left alone regularly can suffer from anxiety and this can lead to:

1  Destructiveness
2  Barking
3  Making messes

Thus right from the very beginning, you

should put the puppy in a play pen or crate and leave him while you are in another part of the house. If he howls and makes a lot of noise, just pop back in and, using your firm voice, make it clear that this is the wrong behaviour. As the puppy learns to settle, you can leave the house for a short period, but always make sure before you leave that everything is safe. Remember that as the puppy becomes house-trained you must arrange for somebody to come in and let the dog out to relieve himself if you are going to be away for more than two or three hours.

## House-training your puppy

■ Puppies, like babies, have no control over their bladders and bowels and need to relieve themselves a lot. There are some obvious times when they need to go outside, e.g. when they first wake up, straight away after eating, and after playing. You soon get used to the

*You can train your puppy to go outside to relieve himself, but newspaper may be useful at night and in emergencies.*

warning signs. For instance, your puppy may wander around sniffing the ground. If this happens, then the first thing to do is to put him outside immediately, rain or shine. You must stay out until the puppy empties himself and then give him a lot of praise.

■ It is often a good idea to always use the same sentence when encouraging your dog – word association can be very useful when the puppy grows up. The trigger sentence can often help when you are in a situation far from home.

■ You can also train your puppy to go to a particular part of the garden each time he relieves himself.

■ Remember that you have a very important role to play in this training, and even though it may take up some of your time initially, it will pay off.

■ The very young puppy will empty

### PLAY BITING

Do not allow your puppy to play bite from an early age. Even little milk teeth are sharp like needles. You must teach the puppy not to do this by giving the command 'No' firmly, and gently pushing him away. The puppy will soon learn an important lesson: that play biting is not allowed and will not gain your attention.

himself almost hourly, and once or twice during the night. As the puppy grows older, he starts to gain bladder control and the message about where he should do the emptying starts to register. Consequently, you will need to go outside with the puppy less frequently.

■ Eventually the puppy will go to the door and, by barking, ask to go out. He will also last throughout the night. If mistakes occur, unless you catch the puppy in the act, it is useless to punish him. He will not understand why you are angry with him. If caught in the act, say 'No' firmly, then pick the puppy up and take him outside to the spot used. If he then obliges, give him lots of praise for going in the correct spot. Punishing after the mistake is no use at all. Never ever hit the puppy or rub his nose in the mess.

■ When your puppy is house-trained, he must be given the chance to empty himself throughout the day, and let out regularly.

## Collar and lead training

You can start this at home during the puppy's vaccination programme before you can take him out for walks. Measure the puppy's neck and buy a lightweight puppy collar and lead from your local pet shop.

■ Start by putting his collar on for 10-15 minutes whilst he is running around. At first, all the puppy will try to do is scratch it off but, after a day or two, he will not even notice it.

■ Then you can attach the lightweight lead and encourage your puppy to walk round the garden with you. At first you might find that it's like a rodeo show with the puppy pulling and jumping. If so, just stop, hold the puppy and say 'No' in your firm voice, and then start again.

■ At the beginning, only attach the lead for five minutes at a time, but each day build it up gradually, adding a few more minutes each time. When the vaccination programme has been completed and the puppy is allowed out of your garden, some of the preliminary work will have been done already.

■ Often when the puppy goes outside, he is so interested in all the things that are going on around him that he will walk well on the lead. When he is ready for his proper collar, you should consider buying a nylon web or rolled leather one with a matching lead. A retractable, flexible extending lead which is 5-10 m long (15-30 ft) is very useful when you cannot let the dog off the lead. You should never buy a choke chain to use as a collar.

## Exercise

Puppies do not need huge amounts of exercise; short walks on the lead to the local park or a field where you can let the puppy have a socialization run around are all that is necessary. You must build up the exercise gradually so that the puppy's muscles are not over-taxed. When your dog is older, he will require longer periods of exercise each day and will not seem to tire. If, for example, you are training for a marathon then you can exercise your dog at the same time. Or if weekends are the time when the whole family goes out for long walks, your dog will be ready to go with you.

## GROOMING

While your puppy is still young and housebound because of his vaccination programme, you should start grooming him every day. Initially, just five minutes' gentle brushing is enough to get him accustomed to being groomed. He will soon start to enjoy the new experience and will welcome these sessions. At the same time, look in his mouth, ears and eyes to make sure that everything is all right (see Chapter 8). The puppy should stand still for you while he is being groomed, and establishing this behaviour now will be useful for later on when you groom him as an adult dog.

*The puppy learns from an early age that your hands are 'kind'. Grooming for a few minutes per day from the beginning makes it easy.*

# FROM THE BEGINNING

Before going into detail about training your dog, we should examine some general environmental features. Retrievers are reasonably large dogs and if they are too boisterous, both in and out of the house, they can become quite a menace. Dogs most commonly become boisterous as a response to their environment, so start as you mean to go on and keep your dog calm from puppyhood onwards. Even when you first bring the puppy home, don't let visitors and children make him over-excited. If he shows signs of excitement, just put him in his pen or crate for a sleep, and tell the children to calm down.

## VOCABULARY FOR YOUR DOG

Keep the vocabulary that you use to your dog very simple, and repeat the same words each time. You should also ensure that the rest of the family use these words. When you are praising him, keep your tone happy and light, but when he has done wrong, use 'No' and 'Bad dog' in a firm, rather than a fierce, tone so that the dog hears and recognises the difference. Retrievers are intelligent dogs, and they want to be praised and to live happily within the family pack. Your dog is a pack animal and you take over from his mother as the pack leader – you must be consistent in this role.

## Control and training

■ Do not let your puppy jump up or climb on the furniture. Give him a firm 'No' and push or put him down so that he is on four feet. Do not throw him down roughly and hurt him.
■ Do not shout at your dog to gain control. Your puppy/dog cannot do something he has not been taught to do.
■ From the beginning the puppy should be trained to: sit, come back when called, and to walk to heel.

## Food and biting

■ Do not feed your dog from the table.
■ Do not your let your dog play bite.
■ You must teach your dog a special command word to let you gently take things out of his mouth. Start doing this from the moment when the puppy arrives; you need not use hardly any pressure at all.

## Leaving your dog

■ From the beginning you should get your puppy accustomed to staying on his own in the house for short periods.
■ Put your puppy into the playpen or crate with a chew toy. Take no notice of

crying or barking – just go and get on with the job in hand.

■ When he is older, you can leave him in the kitchen or utility room, again with a favourite toy or chew stick. Shut the door and either get on with something in the house or go out. Do not leave him alone for too long; gradually increase the time during which he is left.

■ Never leave your puppy or dog on his own with small children or babies.

## Disciplining your dog

■ You must not punish your puppy for anything he does while you are out. He does not understand why you are punishing him after the event.

*All puppies love to play and you should make time each day for this.*

■ If you catch him in the act of doing something wrong, then you can tell him off.

■ Do not hit your puppy or dog with your hand or a stick. It is better to say 'No' firmly and to shake his collar with your hands on either side.

## Barking

■ Do not encourage your dog to bark. If he does bark, do not shout at him to stop. He will think that you are barking too! Instead, give the command 'No, bad dog'. If necessary, you could spray him with water to stop him barking.

# EARLY PUPPY TRAINING

If you have got your puppy used to wearing a collar and lead and he will walk forwards around the garden on his lead, then you have done well. He should also know his name and come when you call him in the garden. Next, you should find a local puppy socialization class where he can meet up and socialize with strange dogs. He must get accustomed to other dogs because he will meet them out in the park and on walks.

This does not mean that you can let him off the lead to be chased by all and sundry, most of whom are completely out of control, untrained and sometimes aggressive. This only serves to make your puppy frightened and disobedient, and later it may lead to aggressive behaviour.

Puppy socialization classes fulfil a useful function. Ask your vet if he knows of any in your area, or look for a notice in your local pet shop or, failing that, contact the Secretary of your breed club.

At these classes, puppies learn to interact with each other and with older dogs. They

learn to read body language and facial and vocal expressions; in this way they can tell other dogs what they want, and they understand what other dogs are telling them.

The atmosphere at these classes is very relaxed, and after play sessions exercises are gradually introduced. The

emphasis is on training for fun, praising the puppy for doing things correctly and providing some food rewards. There is no hard corrective training.

## Obedience courses

As the puppy approaches six months old, he may start the Beginners Obedience Course. This is designed to produce a well-trained dog who is a pleasure to live with – not an Obedience Champion. Retrievers, as sporting dogs, need to do something that will stretch their brains. It is always a good idea to enrol for a short course of obedience training, whatever your objective. Teaching some elementary obedience is helpful for just day-to-day living with your dog.

If you want to work your dog in the field, you may want to take up Obedience, Working Trials or Agility training to a higher level. In the beginning, the UK Kennel Club Good Citizens Test is a good standard to aim for. As part of the Good Citizen Scheme you will receive help in training your dog to be well behaved. This will include advice on grooming, exercise, diet and general health care. The Scheme is open to all dogs, young and old, pedigrees and cross-breeds. At the end of each course a Certificate is awarded to those passing the basic test. There is a Video Guide to the Good Citizen Dog Scheme. For details of training courses and the video contact The Kennel Club (see Useful Addresses, page 144).

*This Retriever is doing what comes naturally to him, but to be a good working dog takes months of training.*

## BEGINNER TRAINING

### Coming when called

■ As you have done the preliminary training with a collar and lead in the garden, the first walk can be a short distance on the lead (up the road and back). Then get in the car and drive to a place where you will let your dog off the lead for a run when he is adult. This should be a large grassy area where it is safe, and not too near a busy road. Check that there are no loose dogs roaming around – you don't want your puppy to be chased by an out-of-control dog. Let the puppy off the lead and allow him to have a little run and sniff before calling him to you.

■ Always take a plastic dog whistle with you. This is obtainable from any pet shop. Practise calling the puppy's name and then blowing three short sharp blasts on the whistle. This is a great saving on your voice and is much easier for the dog to hear. If when you whistle and call, your puppy looks up but doesn't come at once, never run towards him. Instead, run away a little distance and then the puppy will not want to be left and will run after you.

■ When he comes to you, reward him with lots of praise. Never ever hit him or tell him off if he does not come to you straight away. He will then associate coming back with being told off.

> **NOTE**
>
> When training or exercising your dog on the lead always remember to walk your dog on your left-hand side.

■ As you progress with your puppy off the lead, it is sometimes a good idea to reward him with a small titbit.

■ Whilst the puppy is growing, up to six months, do not over exercise him.

## EXERCISE AND TRAINING

Puppies get quite a lot of exercise just playing around. However, they should always have a short walk on the lead and a brief free run once a day. Gradually increase the time until the puppy becomes, at twelve months, a young adult. At this stage, serious obedience and gundog training can be introduced. You have lots of preparatory work to do. Always remember the following guidelines:

■ Never make training sessions too long – fifteen minutes is enough for a young pup.
■ When your dog has completed a task correctly, stop and have a break.
■ If the session is not going well, then go back to something that he has learnt and finish on that.

## The command 'Sit'

■ Say 'Sit' firmly whilst gently pressing your dog's bottom down on to the floor. Each time you say the command, exert a little gentle pressure until he sits. Soon the command word will be followed automatically by the action. Keep the puppy sitting for one minute, then say 'Up' and lavish him with lots of praise when he obeys. You could offer him a titbit, if wished.

■ Alternatively, offer your puppy a titbit, holding it just above his nose. As his head goes back to look at it, his bottom will go down.

## A FEW POINTS TO REMEMBER

- Do not train your puppy for too long at any one time – but do train him every day.
- Do not lose your temper. If you are in a bad mood or your dog is not responding as you wish, stop and have a game instead or just go over something that the dog already knows.
- Dogs, like humans, have different characters, and some like to be treated gently whereas others need firm handling.
- For the early training sessions, choose a quiet place away from other people with no distractions.
- Always finish your lessons on a high note when your dog does something correctly and is rewarded and praised.

## Walking to heel

- Put your puppy's collar and lead on and off you go. By now your puppy should be excited at the prospect of a walk and begin to pull in front of you. Pull the lead back until he is level with you, saying 'Heel' in a firm voice. It's quite a good idea if you can start this exercise with a wall on your left-hand side; this keeps the dog close to you.
- If at the beginning the dog forgets and pulls in front, then do some quick turnabouts and end up facing the right way. This action will bring the dog back to your side. Another good tip is to swing the loose end of the lead in front of the dog's nose as you walk along, but not hitting him with it. If he moves too far ahead, the swinging lead will just touch his nose and he will move back.

## Walking to heel off the lead

- When your dog walks well to heel on the lead you can start training him to walk to heel off the lead. Set off as normal, then drop the lead and keep on walking. Afterwards, if he stays by your side, give him lots of praise. Always keep encouraging the dog to heel by tapping your left thigh with your left hand.

## Stay

■ When you have perfected the 'Sit' command, stand in front of your dog and give him the command word 'Sit'. Move a stride away and say 'Stay' slowly and firmly.

■ Gradually increase the distance between you. If the dog moves towards you, go back and ask him to 'sit' on the original spot. Praise him and only move away a short distance.

■ Change your direction, but do not always go the same way. Walk round the dog but at this early stage always go back to him rather than calling him to come to you. The dog must have a clear idea of what you want.

## Come

■ Your puppy has learnt to come when you call and whistle when he is off the lead. Now after learning 'Sit-stay' it's time for him to learn to come to you from this position.

■ Walk backwards about twenty yards. Repeating the word 'Stay', keep walking back. Go back to your dog and praise him.

■ Once again ask him to 'Sit', then 'Stay', and walk away about twenty yards. Stop and call your dog, using his name and the whistle. Walking back and praising your dog, and then walking away again and calling him prevents your dog anticipating your command. After two or three weeks of this, your dog should walk to heel, and sit, stay and come to you on command.

### IMPORTANT

Remember throughout the training process that all dogs are individuals and learn at different speeds.

## HOLIDAYS AND TRAVEL

### ■ Holiday care

You must make proper arrangements for your dog if you go away on holiday. Asking a neighbour to pop in and feed your dog and let him out will not do. Make enquiries about good boarding kennels in your area — your vet may be able to suggest some. It is important that you inspect them before you leave your dog in their care.

Look for bright, alert staff, clean premises and happy dogs. In turn, the kennels may wish to see your dog's vaccination certificate and ask you lots of questions about your dog. You should do your investigations and book your dog in well ahead of your holiday, as the best kennels do get booked up.

### ■ Travelling in the car

From the very beginning, you should take your puppy out in the car to get him used to car travel. For safety's sake, you should fit a dog guard (one that your dog cannot wriggle through!) or use a crate for transporting your dog. Never leave your dog in the car in hot weather as the temperature rises rapidly. Even in cool weather, you should leave a window open for your dog.

## RETRIEVING

1 For this practice it is usual to buy a small canvas lightweight green dummy. Any good pet shop will order one for you. Ask the puppy to 'Sit, stay', then throw the dummy.

2 Restrain the puppy for a second, then send him to retrieve the dummy, using a command such as 'Go fetch'. As the puppy picks it up, give the command 'Come' and blow your whistle as the dog brings it to you.

3 Gently take it out of his mouth, giving the command 'Dead'. This is a useful way of taking something off a Retriever, including the many things they carry around the house.

### Staying whilst the dummy is thrown

■ You do not want your puppy to think that everything thrown is to be retrieved at once. He must learn to be steady. Make the puppy sit on the lead if you wish, then throw the dummy but do not let the puppy dash off after it. Say 'No' and then go and retrieve it yourself.

■ Let the puppy fetch the next dummy or the third one, but you should always finish on a dog fetch.

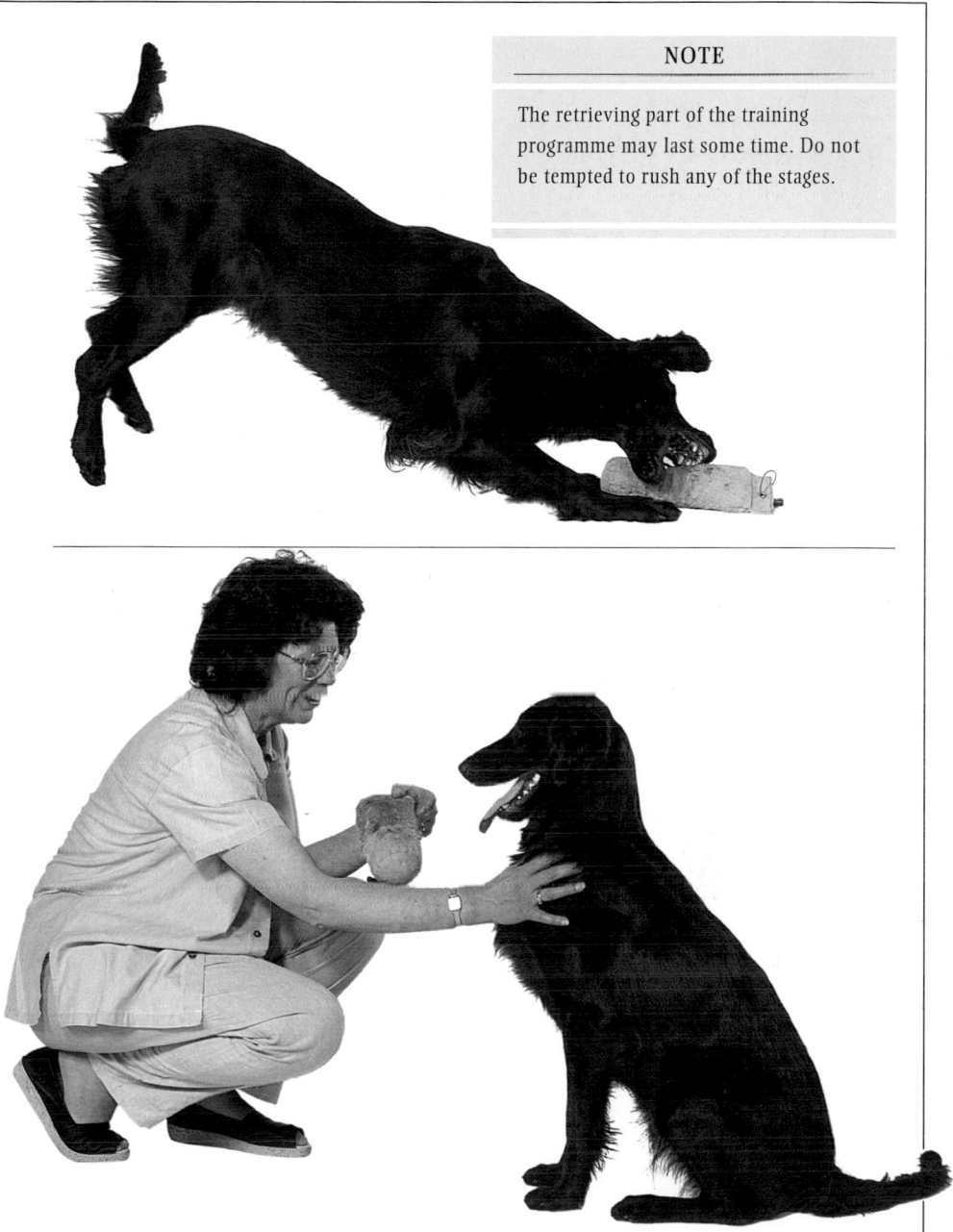

**NOTE**

The retrieving part of the training programme may last some time. Do not be tempted to rush any of the stages.

# PART TWO

# CARING FOR YOUR DOG

Buying any puppy or acquiring an adult dog is a huge responsibility, and caring for any dog will take up a lot of your time over the next ten or so years. Therefore it is not a decision to be taken lightly but one that requires careful consideration by all the members of your family. Retriever puppies can look especially appealing but they should never be bought on impulse. Many people forget that these cute little creatures grow up into large dogs. Retrievers make good companions and loving family pets as well as working gundogs, but they need a great deal of exercise and lots of your attention. In this section on caring for your dog, you will find expert advice on choosing a puppy and looking after him; feeding, exercising and grooming your adult dog; breeding from your dog; and also how you can both enjoy the experience of showing your dog.

# CHAPTER FOUR

# BUYING AND CARING FOR A PUPPY

## CHOOSING A PUPPY

Once you and your family have decided that you want a Retriever, the next important step is where you go to get a puppy. It's not like going to the supermarket straight away and getting something off the shelf. A puppy is a living being who will grow in size and needs as much attention at the beginning as a new baby. If he is treated properly and sensibly, he will add considerably to the quality of your life.

The way in which your puppy has been reared is a very important factor in your choice as you take your first step towards owning a Retriever.

### Puppy farms

If you purchase a puppy from a large pet-selling complex which buys in puppies, it is impossible for you to see the pup's mother. The puppies in these places often come in bulk from puppy farms, or from unsuitable breeders who have not been able to sell the puppies themselves. Frequently, these puppies have been sent on very long journeys in too small a container. They may have been fed incorrectly from the beginning, just as their mother would be, because the aim of these puppy farms is to spend as little money as possible and to make the maximum profit. To compound the faults, these puppies are usually reared in cramped quarters. The sires and dams very rarely have their hips or eyes checked and thus the puppies may inherit genetic disorders. With this type of sale, you are buying trouble and helping to perpetuate an unsavoury business. However, people do buy these puppies and of course they do grow fond of them when they take them home. If a problem is quickly perceived and the puppy does not seem to be a viable proposition after all, it is difficult to send him back, and right from the start you may be paying out expensive vets' fees.

*All puppies look very appealing but you should only buy a Retriever if you have the space, financial commitment and time for such a dog.*

## Finding a breeder

If you are buying a Retriever and have no idea of where to go for one, then you should contact the Kennel Club (see Useful Addresses, page 144) and ask for the names and addresses of the Club Secretaries of either the Golden Retrievers, Flat Coated Retrievers or Curly Coated Retrievers.

If your heart is set on a Golden Retriever, you can ask for the Secretary of the area nearest to you. There are thirteen Golden Retriever Clubs covering most areas in Great Britain. Flat Coats and Curly Coated Retrievers do not have so many clubs.

The Club Secretary will be able to put you in touch with a breeder near your home who has a litter with some available puppies or who has a litter due, or even knows of a litter by their stud dog. Most clubs have codes of ethics which their members agree to abide by. These codes are designed to help protect the general health of any puppies. Most small specialist breeders are breeding to continue their lines and

### LOCAL SOURCES

You may see a nice looking dog locally and be able to find out the name of the breeder. Alternatively, your local vet will often be able to tell you of any puppies if one of his clients has a litter.

their puppies will be fed and reared correctly, socialized and often inoculated.

## Dog or bitch?

This is an important decision, although in these days of spaying females the season aspect is of less importance than it used to be. Nowadays, many vets recommend that you allow the bitch to have one season and then spay her. However, it is often forgotten that this is a relatively major operation which can have detrimental effects on the dog's coat etc.

As the male retriever is just as loving and as pleasant in temperament as the bitch, it is often better to have a dog, although there is a size difference, females being slightly smaller. The old saying that dogs tend to stray after bitches in season should have no bearing on your dog's lifestyle and the decision you make. No responsible owner will let their dog out to stray, and your garden should be properly fenced and escape-proof.

If you buy a bitch, remember that she will come into season about once every nine months, and during this time she must be watched to ensure that she does not come into contact with loose male dogs. For obvious reasons, you should keep her on the lead during the twenty-one day period. Remember that any discharge can stain carpets and upholstery so take steps to protect your furniture from accidents.

## Should you have a dog?

Before you buy a dog, you should consider carefully whether it's a sensible thing to do. As the saying goes, a dog is not only for Christmas; in fact, the dog you get will become your companion for the next twelve years or so. All dogs, especially the intelligent Retrievers, need a lot of your time and effort from the moment you bring your new puppy home. However, you will reap the benefits with your dog over and over again.

■ First of all, ask yourself honestly whether you are prepared to change your lifestyle. Dogs need lots of regular exercise, games and attention.

■ Do all your family want a puppy? It is

*It's not easy to choose when presented with a litter of lovable puppies. It is often best to opt for a bold, sociable dog.*

important that everybody wants a dog, and not just you or the children. If your children are frightened of dogs, or your partner thinks a dog can be kept in the garage, then you shouldn't get one. If your dog is going to lead to arguments and the main sufferer will be the puppy, then you shouldn't get one. If the children want a puppy, only buy one if they are prepared to help look after him and you are happy to be involved.

■ Do not be misled by seeing well-trained adult dogs or puppies who are

49

responding well to training. It takes work and dedication to train a dog and you must not under-estimate the amount of time you will have to invest in this.

■ A dog is not inexpensive to keep, and you will need to invest in a collar, lead, basket, toys and grooming equipment as well as feeding a growing puppy. You will have to pay for inoculations, worming treatments and vets' bills.

■ Puppies need a lot of attention – you cannot go out to work all day and expect a puppy to look after himself. Dogs are social pack animals and it is cruel to leave them on their own for long periods. Lonely,

*Most Retrievers enjoy obedience and agility training. This dog is bringing back a canvas dummy over a jump.*

bored puppies become mischievous, and destructive adults. Don't buy a dog if you spend a lot of time away from home.

■ Retrievers are intelligent dogs with boundless energy and need regular daily exercise, whatever the weather or however busy your schedule. Only get one if you are prepared to set aside some time each day for exercising your dog.

■ If you have young children, they will have to learn respect for the puppy: that he is not a mechanical toy to be battered and then thrown to one side. Children can be cruel and you must make sure that they are gentle with the puppy.

■ Another consideration is the size of your house and garden. Retrievers are relatively big dogs and they need space. You must ensure that your garden is fenced securely so that your dog cannot escape. Also, if you are a proud gardener, you must be prepared for the odd incident when your dog proudly brings you the flowers he has dug up!

## Choosing an older dog

You may even decide for many different reasons that you would rather have an older dog than a young puppy of less than six months. Buying an older dog does have some advantages for people who feel that they cannot cope with house-training and all the destructive chewing stages of puppyhood.

However, the dog will have been trained by somebody else to their ways or perhaps not trained at all. He may be very set in his own canine behaviour and habits, many of which you may have to change. You should not consider taking on a dog like this if you have never owned a dog before.

To get an older dog, you should contact the Breed Club Secretaries and they will put you in touch with the Rescue Co-ordinator for your breed. The

### CHOOSING A WORKING DOG

If you wish to work your Retriever in the field, then you should contact a breeder of working dogs. All Retrievers have some working instincts, but if you want to train your dog to work with you in the field you should look for a dog with the right bloodlines. Some puppies are descended from long lines of dogs who have been bred for their biddability, style and speed. You can train most Retrievers to compete successfully in agility, obedience and working competitions and also in straightforward picking up and going out shooting with you. However, if you want to enter the specialized world of Field Trials you would be well advised to buy a dog with working lines.

breed rescue will know why the dog needs re-homing, and will have assessed his needs. Be prepared to be quizzed regarding your suitability to own the dog; he will come to you on a trial basis.

Dogs come into rescue centres for many reasons, not just because of ill-treatment. Marriage breakdowns, the death of an owner and a change in family circumstances are all common reasons.

Sometimes a breeder has an adult dog which is available for re-homing. In this case find out as much as possible about the dog and have him for a trial period before making a final decision.

## BRINGING YOUR PUPPY HOME

When you have made the decision to buy a dog, have found a reputable breeder and have chosen a puppy, you will probably be asked many questions by the breeder before you can bring your puppy home. A responsible breeder will be concerned about the puppies' welfare and will want to ensure that they will have good homes. Be prepared to answer a lot of questions about your lifestyle, the size of your home and garden, your job and the amount of time you can give your puppy.

For your part, you must also assure yourself that the puppies have been bred responsibly and have been adequately socialized in the breeder's home. Most puppies leave their litter at the age of about eight weeks old. When the time comes to pick your puppy up, it is a good idea to choose a Saturday so that everybody in the family is at home while he is settling in and exploring his new home.

The breeder should already have given you a diet sheet so that you can buy some of the puppy's food in advance. Most stomach problems are caused by changing a puppy's usual diet and the type of food to which he has become accustomed. If, after a few days, you wish to change the

pup's food, only introduce the new food gradually, adding a little at a time to the food you are giving until eventually you change over completely to the new food.

Before you bring the puppy home, you must decide where he is going to live and sleep in your house. No puppy should be kept outside alone in a kennel. It is the interaction between the puppy and the humans in his pack that makes dog-owning so enjoyable.

## SOCIALIZATION

One reason why you should buy your puppy from a small private breeder is that the socialization and handling of puppies from an early age is vital to what the adult dog becomes. The mother teaches the puppies much of their behaviour and as they play they learn what is permissible behaviour and what is not allowed.

Your family or one particular member of it, will take over from the puppy's mother as pack leader. Also of great importance from baby puppyhood is gentle handling by humans. Of course, one has to be careful not to introduce infection, but the caring breeder will check that the people who handle the puppies are very careful.

You might find when you first go to see the litter that you walk through a disinfectant tray to prevent spreading germs to the mother and puppies.

## Playpens

You must have somewhere from the very beginning in which you can put the puppy so that he is safe and out of the way of the family. The best place is a puppy pen, which is just the same as a baby's playpen. You can buy puppy panels that clip together, and you will need a minimum of four, but you can buy more if you want a larger pen.

The playpen can be set up in the kitchen or any room without a carpet. Provide a piece of vet bed at one end on which the puppy can sleep, and cover the rest of the floor with newspapers. If you are good at woodwork, you can make your own framework of wood and fill in the sides with sheets of strong 2.5-cm (1-in) metal mesh. The holes should not be too large or the puppy could get his paws or head caught. The pen must be strong enough to stay upright if the puppy jumps up against it, and the panels should be 105 x 90 cm (42 x 36 in).

A playpen is useful at so many times. It is a place where the puppy can rest or sleep; where you can put him out of the way of visitors or very small children who are just starting to toddle. You can leave him in it safely while you are preparing food and you don't want the puppy under your feet. It is also a good idea to leave the puppy in it for short periods if you are going out.

An alternative to a playpen is a

metal dog crate, which can be obtained from most pet shops. Crates are quite expensive and look like a large fold-down box made of welded steel. They come in different sizes, and you must buy a size that is suitable for an adult Retriever so that he is able to stand upright and turn around in it. If you do opt for a crate, you will need a large one of about 104 x 64 x 68 cm (41 x 25 x 27 in).

These crates are very useful later on if you travel a lot with your puppy or adult dog. They can be put in a bedroom for the dog to sleep in and can also be useful in caravans. They can be used in estate cars, hatchbacks or vans, and fold down easily and can be carried by their special handle. One thing you should always remember with a crate is that it is not a place where a puppy or an adult dog should be locked away for hours on end as a prisoner. Do not leave a puppy in a crate for longer then one hour; no

## BEDDING

This will last from puppyhood into adulthood, and the ideal bedding is made from a fleecy machine-washable fabric developed in hospitals. It is sold under many brand names and your pet shop will be able to get it for you. You should buy a piece that is large enough for an adult to lie down comfortably. Get three pieces: one in use, one ready to be used and one being washed. They dry very quickly, and absorb water and dirt when in use – qualities that make them invaluable.

more than two hours for an adult dog.

A crate or playpen can also be useful if you already have an older dog. If you want him to live in harmony with the new puppy, you will need a safe place where you can put the puppy for short periods to give the older dog some peace.

## Preparing for your puppy

When you are ready to pick up the puppy you should be prepared and ready for his arrival in your home.

■ The safe pen or crate should be ready for the puppy.

■ You should have a supply of the puppy's usual food together with some puppy food dishes and a stronger bowl for water.

■ Buy some safe puppy toys from the pet shop. A one-litre plastic milk bottle, washed out and the screwtop thrown away, makes a good Retriever toy.

■ When you pick up your puppy, take some newspaper and a towel with you in the car in case the puppy is travel sick, (although this should not happen as the breeder will not feed a puppy before making a journey).

■ Remember to ask for a puppy diet sheet if the breeder forgets to give you one.

■ A pedigree registration form should be obtained from the Kennel Club and completed and sent back straight away. This will enable you to transfer the puppy into your name, which also means that he will be insured for a number of weeks.

Insurance is always sensible and it is better to be safe than sorry. There are a few insurance companies that specialize in pet insurance and you can obtain further information about this from your vet when you arrange the vaccination programme.

## The first hour in your home

As soon as you arrive home after the journey, you should let the puppy run around your safe, securely fenced garden until he empties himself. This is the first part of the house-training programme: always go outside.

Right from the beginning, if you have children, they must be educated to treat the puppy properly. He is not a toy or just a plaything, but a living creature, and children must be taught to have a responsible attitude to him. Picking him up incorrectly, hugging him too tightly and dropping him can all be harmful to a small puppy.

Remember that puppies tend to play and run around fast for short periods and then want to sleep. So show the puppy around the parts of the house in which he will live. Do not allow him to climb the stairs at this stage. If necessary, use a baby gate as a temporary precaution at the bottom of the stairs.

Allow the puppy to play for a while, then feed him what he would be normally eating at that time of day, according to the diet sheet. Put him outside again to empty himself and then into the pen or crate to sleep.

He may cry a little but he will soon

*Your new puppy will set out on a voyage of discovery at eight weeks when he leaves the litter.*

settle down. While he is sleeping get on with your chores before he awakens. If you have an older dog, remember that he didn't ask you to get a puppy! You can introduce them by holding the puppy and let the other dog sniff him all over. Then put the puppy down on the floor and make a great fuss of the older dog. Continue to fuss over the older dog until the puppy is absorbed into the household. Don't make the mistake of

## SLEEPING

The first night, the puppy might wake up in the middle of the night and bark. Make sure that he is warm and has not got too large an area in which to wander around; a puppy pen or crate is ideal. He will soon go back to sleep again and will settle into a routine at night. Of course, he will be lonely at first: he has left the only life he knew with his brothers and sisters. However, he will forget about his litter-mates and will settle down into the routine of your home and living in a new pack – your family.

just becoming besotted with the new puppy and ignoring your older dog; this would cause jealousy.

## Feeding your puppy

A responsible breeder will give you a diet sheet for the puppy with instructions on how to feed him when you take him home and in the weeks ahead. All puppies need to be fed small amounts of food at regular times, usually four or five times a day with the first meal early in the morning and the last meal at bedtime. A full stomach at night will help the puppy to sleep well. As an example, you could feed him at 8am, midday, 4pm, 8pm and, finally, at 11pm. As the puppy grows, the number of meals can be gradually reduced to three meals, and then to one large or two smaller meals as an adult dog.

■ **What to feed**

There is a wide range of food available for puppies, including complete dried foods, canned foods and biscuit meal, and prepared meat. Also, you can prepare and cook fresh meat for your dog, in which case it must be combined with

special puppy biscuit meal to ensure that he gets a balanced diet containing all the nutrients he needs. The advantage of feeding him commercially prepared puppy foods is that they are devised specifically to provide him with the correct nutrition.

The food requirement for a growing puppy is, weight for weight, greater than that of a normal adult dog. Just follow the instructions on the can or packet, or ask your vet for advice. If you are feeding fresh meat to your puppy, he will need 420 g (14 oz) per day, which can be divided equally between four or five meals. He will also need 50 g (2 oz) biscuit meal or mixer to be split between the meals.

You must not give a young puppy of seven to eight weeks any cow's milk as it contains a lot of milk sugar lactose and may cause diarrhoea. Your puppy will have been fed up until now on his mother's milk and what he needs is a special milk powder designed for dogs. This can be obtained from most pet shops and can be prepared and mixed according to the manufacturer's instructions.

Your puppy will also need to have a continuous supply of water, which should be changed or topped up as necessary throughout the day. If he is on a complete diet, his need for water will increase.

When you bring your puppy home, his motions may be a little loose for the first couple of days, especially if you were not given a diet sheet and he is

*You should let the puppy have his own proper playthings. Otherwise he will improvise with your shoes and other household or personal items.*

eating different food from usual. Don't worry about this; he will soon settle down. However, if the diarrhoea continues, you should consult your vet.

## Equipment

A new puppy will need quite a lot of equipment, although this need not be very expensive. There are some items that you must buy.

### ■ Collar

A very young puppy can wear a soft puppy collar for short periods to get used to it around his neck. His neck size will grow rapidly and it won't be long before he needs a larger collar. Remember that collars should not be too loose nor too tight. From about six months of age, the puppy can wear a leather or webbing collar. Gundogs look very smart in olive green webbing collars.

### ■ Lead

Your puppy will need a lead to attach to his collar. Start out with a lightweight puppy one and invest in a stronger one when he gets older. An extending lead may be a good buy as it is helpful in training the puppy and enables him to roam over quite a large area in parks and public places where you may not wish to let him off the lead.

### ■ Feeding bowl

For your puppy's first feeding bowl, it is best to buy a plastic one.

# CHAPTER FIVE

# CARING FOR AN ADULT DOG

People are becoming more aware of the importance of a well balanced diet for themselves and their family and this also colours their attitude towards feeding their dog. You want to maintain your Retriever's fitness and health, but how do you choose between all the different brands and foods on the shelves of your local pet shop or supermarket?

It is a myth that dogs get bored eating the same food day after day. Dogs do not need to taste different flavours to enjoy their food, and changing their usual diet can actually cause diarrhoea.

The digestive tract of the dog is short and the digestive process is simple. Food passes through quickly and therefore it must be easily digested. The food is eaten quickly because dogs, unlike humans, do not chew or grind the food in their mouth. Their intestine is short, about 4 m (12 ft), and it cannot cope with large volumes of food. Moreover, the food has only a short time to undergo digestion. Although dogs have quite a large stomach, it can stretch and predispose them to gastric dilation and torsion (bloat).

## Dog foods

There is a great variety of foods available for dogs, ranging from commercially canned and dried foods to the food you prepare at home. Your dog relies on you for an appropriate diet to keep him fit and healthy. Dogs are naturally carnivorous, meaning that they have a preference for food of animal origin. However, wild dogs also eat the stomach of their prey, which contains vegetable matter as well. Thus only feeding meat to your dog would be unbalanced as well as expensive, for roughage is an essential part of a dog's diet.

## Complete foods

As the label says, 'complete' means that the food contains the correct balance of

*This Flat Coated Retriever is alert and waiting for his owner's command. All Retrievers are very biddable.*

protein, animal and vegetable fats (both saturated and unsaturated) as well as carbohydrates, fibre, minerals and vitamins. The balance can be adjusted to suit the individual dog's needs for growth, reproduction, maintenance and activity. You need to follow the instructions as to the amount and the type needed for your dog, depending on whether he is a growing puppy, a teenager, a mature dog, an elderly dog, a working dog or a fat dog.

*Most Retrievers enjoy swimming and love to retrieve things, such as toys and dummies, from water.*

Complete foods all look different. They may include flaked ingredients or pellets – some may be a mixture of both. Most can be fed soaked or dry, although many dogs seem to find the soaked sort more palatable.

■ **Advantages of complete foods**

**1** You do not need to give the dog any extra additives.

**2** You do not need to mix separate foods.

**3** Complete foods are easy to prepare and to store.

**Note:** whatever type of food you decide to feed your dog, you must provide a bowl of water for him at all times. This should be

topped up as necessary. However, on a complete diet, it is even more essential that dogs get plenty to drink.

■ **Disadvantages of complete foods**

**1** Dogs who are fed complete foods tend to excrete a larger amount of faeces than dogs on other diets.

**2** As they drink a lot of water, which is essential, they tend to produce more urine.

## Special ranges

There are diet ranges that contain no artificial colourings, flavourings and preservatives. You can also buy some vegetarian foods for dogs.

### TRADITIONAL FEEDING

The other method of feeding dogs is to provide home-cooked fresh meat, tripe, canned meat or dried meat plus a good-quality biscuit meal. To complete the balance you need to supplement your dog's diet with the right minerals and vitamins. Herbal additives are very popular nowadays.

The biscuit meal should be soaked for about two hours until it is twice its original size, soft and ready to be mixed with the meat. As a guide, an active young Retriever should receive 350 g (12 oz) biscuit meal plus 450 g (1 lb) meat. Some of the biscuits, approximately 115 g (4 oz) can be fed as hard dog biscuits at the opposite end of the day to the main meal.

## Bones

Dogs enjoy chewing large marrow bones. They help to keep their teeth clean. You can also buy snack bones in pet shops.

## Choosing the right food

Some people have lots of time for food preparation and enjoy planning their dog's diet and doing all the weighing, cutting and cooking. Others prefer to follow a diet plan with everything worked out for them. You'll know if you are feeding your dog correctly. A healthy dog eating a balanced diet should have a glossy coat, elastic-feeling skin, bright eyes and be ready for anything. He should not be too fat, nor too thin with the ribs showing very obviously.

## Exercise

Regular exercise helps to keep your dog healthy. It is one of the best aspects of dog ownership, but must be done every day whatever the weather. Do not ever think that exercising consists of merely opening the door to let your dog roam the streets. Nor is it just letting your dog out into the garden – that is not exercise. A Retriever needs a thirty-minute walk on the lead, morning and evening, followed by a good run and sniff around off the lead in a safe place.

You must be responsible and pick up your dog's mess. You can take a plastic bag and a little plastic scoop with you for this purpose.

*An active, healthy Retriever must have a certain amount of free running off the lead every day.*

## Grooming and bathing

Grooming is an essential part of keeping your Retriever in top-class condition. If you started grooming from an early age and brushed your puppy every day, he should be used to the experience and will even enjoy it. Keep on with this daily grooming session and then your dog's coat will be free of tangles.

Bathing your Retriever once a year is usually sufficient. However, if he rolls in something 'smelly', then additional baths may be necessary. In the bath or shower, use a rubber mat so that the dog does not scratch the base. If the weather is warm, you can bath him in an old-fashioned metal tub or bath outside, or even on some concrete with a shower attachment on the tap.

The water should only be as warm as you would use to wash a baby – not too hot nor too cold. Always use a specially formulated dog shampoo. Lather it up and then wash it out thoroughly. Rub your dog dry with a towel or use a hair dryer. However, if using this method, check that you are not blowing hot air on to the dog's skin. Finish off with a grooming session and then run a comb through the dog's coat.

## Your veteran Retriever

As your dog ages, you may need to modify his diet and exercise and make small adjustments to his normal daily routine and the way in which you care for him. Here are a few useful guidelines. You must remember to:

■ Keep your dog warm. Many dogs suffer from rheumatism in old age.

■ Watch out that you do not let your old dog get too fat. Overweight dogs are less likely to be as healthy or to live as long. If you are concerned about your dog's weight, ask your vet for advice.

■ Some dogs prefer to eat two smaller meals rather than one large one as they get older.

### EUTHANASIA

If the time comes that your vet advises you that the quality of your dog's life is not what it should be, then you may have to make a difficult decision. If you decide on euthanasia, stay with your dog and hold him in your arms when the vet gives him the final injection. Your dog has been part of your family and your devoted companion.

■ Give your dog as much exercise as he can do comfortably.

■ Keep your dog well groomed and trimmed – don't neglect him just because he is now a veteran.

# 6

# BREEDING

## DECIDING TO BREED

If you are thinking of breeding from your dog because someone told you that every bitch needs at least one litter for her health's sake, then forget it. This just isn't true. If you are planning to have a litter, there are some questions you must answer first, and honestly. First, why do you want to breed from your bitch – to make money? This reason will not stand up and has a built-in downwards spiral. The specific breed rescue organisations are full of the results of unknowledgeable, uncaring so-called 'breeders' who thought they could make money out of breeding. Many of these people are prepared to sell their puppies to anybody who is willing to pay the asking price.

Some people just want another dog and decide to breed from their bitch as a way of getting a puppy. However, it is easier just to buy another puppy. Other people get involved in breeding after taking up showing their pet dog as an enjoyable hobby. They decide that they would like to start a strain of their own. This is fine in principle but breeding carries its own responsibilities. Breeders

bring puppies into the world and their involvement does not always end when they sell them. They must be prepared to help if at any stage the dog they have sold cannot be kept by the new owners.

### Considerations for new breeders

Before you breed your first litter, you must consider the following points.

**1** You must breed only from healthy stock and that means you must get your bitch's hips X-rayed for Hip Dysplasia and scored under the B.A scheme (see Chapter 9). If she has more than the breed average score, then you must not breed from her. Golden Retrievers also have their eyes examined yearly for eye problems. Again, if your dog is found to have any eye problems you cannot use her for breeding. The dog you use at stud must also have a low hip score and, if he is a Golden, up-to-date eye certificates.

**2** Whelping a bitch and looking after the puppies correctly is very time consuming. You just cannot go out to work in the morning and come back at night to your bitch and puppies. Weaned puppies need to be fed little and often at the beginning,

and must be given five meals every day.
**3** Another consideration is how you house the puppies and whether you have enough space. Puppies do not spend eight weeks only in the small area of the whelping box. You need a quiet place in which the bitch can whelp, and it must be kept at the correct temperature. You must also have adequate facilities for the bitch and her litter for the first four weeks of puppyhood, and then increased space until the puppies leave at eight weeks.
**4** You will never make a fortune out of breeding. In fact, at the beginning you will be spending a lot of money on stud fees, registration fees, good food for the bitch and puppies and, if bad luck strikes, vets' fees. You should get this money back and even make a small profit when the puppies are sold, but if you work out how much your time is worth and how much time you have spent on the litter, you would probably be in debit.
**5** You will have to sell your puppies to suitable homes so ask yourself a few questions. Have you a list of suitable

people who want your puppies? How do you know if people are suitable?

Remember all those questions the breeder of your dog asked you before you knew you could definitely have a puppy. What if a puppy sale falls through at eight weeks? Can you keep that puppy until another suitable buyer comes along? If you can't sell all the puppies, can you afford to keep them and wait for the right owner to come along? Remember that the older the puppies are, the harder they are to sell.

## How to choose your stud dog

Your bitch will be typical of the breed in appearance and temperament: kindly, friendly and confident with several generations in her pedigree with clear eye certificates and good hip scores. You will probably be able to ask the breeder of your bitch for advice on which stud dog to use. However, he needs to have the same requirements in order to breed from him. You must consider the physical attributes of the dog you are thinking of using.

Genetics play an important role in finding the right dog. Genes are the unique individual patterns that all animals carry in the cells of their bodies. It is genes that determine what an animal will look like and will also decide how the animal will behave. Genes are carried in the body on strings known as chromosomes, of which dogs have thirty-nine pairs. A puppy inherits half its genes from the sire and half from the

dam. However, a dog with a very short muzzle mated to a bitch with a very long muzzle, will not produce the perfect one. Not all genes are equal; there are dominant and recessive genes. Dominant genes show in the dog or bitch, whereas recessive genes are there but hidden and only show when a mating takes place with a dog or bitch who also carries the gene as a recessive. Physically you want the dog you use to complement your bitch and not fail in the points where she has weaknesses. However, this does not mean that you must only use a show champion or champion sire.

## In-breeding

This involves mating animals together who are very closely related, such as a father and daughter, a mother and son, or a brother and sister. By doing this, you are not introducing fresh blood. Indeed, this way you fix the virtues, but bring out hidden faults. In-breeding is only for the breeder who knows about all the virtues and failings of the dogs on the pedigree. It doubles and triples on the bad as well as the good. Well known successful breeders often have permutations which they use: a bitch to her litter brother's best son, a half-brother and sister mating, or a bitch back to her grandfather. If you wish to in-breed, both the dog and bitch must be of true type and excellent specimens of the breed.

### LINE BREEDING

This means mating your bitch to a dog of the same family lines. To do this, you go back on the top lines to the same very good dog or bitch. Your puppies' pedigree will go back to this dog or bitch five or six times in five generations. This is a very popular and successful method, but the dog or bitch with whom you line breed must have been outstanding, and the method must have worked well with other bitches of your bloodlines.

Remember that you are going to have to take things on trust about this outstanding dog or bitch because he or she will now be old or dead. You will often find that the great strains in your breed are line bred into their own strains.

## Outcrossing

This type of breeding is when you mate a bitch to a dog who is not related to her. No dogs are the same on a given generation pedigree but they are both registered as Golden, Flat Coated or Curly Coated Retrievers. You must find common ancestors if you research back far enough but they would have no influence on your breeding. It is said that you have bred a 'sport' if you get one superb animal from this type of mating. However, they rarely breed on with their own excellence. You cannot line breed on to fix type.

## HEREDITARY CONDITIONS

Both the dog and bitch must, if Golden Retrievers, have current eye certificates. All Retrievers, both dogs and bitches, must have been hip scored under the BVA scheme and be no more than the breed average. You must show your certificates and see those of the stud dog before the mating. Likewise, you must check that the bitch has a correct mouth, dentition-wise.

## Mating guidelines

**1** You must decide on and make the arrangements for which stud dog you wish to use, well in advance of the bitch coming into season.

**2** It is best to mate a bitch when she is about two years old, her third season. She must not be mated before this as she is still growing. In the UK, you cannot mate a bitch over eight years without obtaining special permission from the Kennel Club. A bitch would never be mated for the first time if she is more than five to six years old. Moreover, whatever her age, she must be in excellent condition.

**3** Contact the breeder of your bitch for their advice on which stud dog to use. Alternatively, contact the Secretary of your nearest breed club if you cannot get in touch with your bitch's breeder.

**4** Contact the owner of the dog, and ask whether you can have his pedigree. Has he got all his up-to-date certificates and is he at public stud? What is the stud fee? In turn, you will be asked questions about your bitch. If everything is all right on both sides, you can book the dog and will be asked to get in touch when your bitch first comes in season. You should contact the owner of the stud dog when your bitch first comes in season, not on her tenth day but at the beginning.

## The oestrus cycle

There are four phases in the bitch's oestrus cycle. They are as follows:

**1 Anoestrus:** the time of sexual inactivity.

**2 Pro-oestrus:** the start of vaginal bleeding. The bitch cannot usually be mated at this stage.

**3 Oestrus:** the bitch's time of acceptance of the male. The vaginal discharge can become colourless at this time.

**4 Metoestrus:** the stage that occurs in the unmated bitch.

## MAKE ALLOWANCES

We have a saying in my family that our dogs have never read a book on breeding and always do things slightly differently! Books can only describe the norm, and your bitch might not conform exactly.

## MATING

Before you mate your bitch you must decide where everything is going to take place on the big day.

### Where will your bitch whelp?

This should always be in comfortable accommodation where she is used to staying. Never build a kennel in the garden and put her in it the day before she whelps, nor should you bring a bitch who lives outside into the house the night before she whelps. Remember that you will be with your bitch throughout the whelping and you need to be comfortable too with all the facilities you need. The birth must take place in a quiet place where the bitch will be completely relaxed – a utility room is ideal.

### Your bitch in season

The warning signs that your bitch is coming into season are as follows:
■ She may pass frequent small amounts of urine when she is out exercising.
■ The vulva will start to swell.
■ It is very easy to miss the start of the season so check for any blood-stained discharge by gently pressing a white tissue against the bitch's vulva morning and evening.

From the beginning of the season, the bitch must be kept away from all male dogs and should be exercised on the lead, even though in the early stages she cannot be mated. On the first day of the season, telephone the owner of the stud dog to arrange when to take her over for mating.

### Advice on mating

1 You will have arranged to arrive at the stud dog's house at a specific time.

#### THE BEST TIME FOR MATING

The twelfth to the fourteenth day from when the bitch comes into season is the norm for mating, although times may vary. The physical signs that the bitch is ready are as follows:
■ An enlarged vulva that gets softer.
■ The discharge becomes straw coloured rather than blood stained.
■ When you stroke the bitch down her spine and the base of her tail, she will start to move her tail slightly to one side.
■ There are other ways of telling when a bitch is ready to be mated using veterinary science. The vet will take a vaginal smear from your bitch and will repeat this over several days. Looking at the types of cell present and the amount of them, your vet can discern the stage of the bitch's cycle. A series of smears will be taken at forty-eight hourly intervals, to identify the correct day.

## BLOOD TEST METHOD

A blood test is sometimes taken between the seventh and tenth days to measure the progesterone levels in the blood. The test is repeated until the result shows that the bitch is starting oestrus and is ready to mate within twenty-four hours, or is ready for mating immediately. Many bitches fail to conceive because they have been mated too early, so it is important to establish the right time for mating.

However, allow a little extra time and be early so that you can stop to let your bitch urinate.

**2** Ensure that your bitch is wearing a proper collar – you may need to hold her steady during the mating, so on no account take her on just a slip lead.

**3** Remember that this is something new to your bitch and although she may be even-tempered, she may find it quite a frightening experience.

**4** The ideal situation is that the dog and bitch get to know each other by playing together in a large spacious area for quite a long time before mating spontaneously.

**5** However, if you go to an experienced stud dog this is not what usually happens. Never leave your bitch to be mated while you wait in another room. Your bitch will be happier and more confident if you are there with her during the mating.

**6** Usually you will accompany your bitch to where the mating will take place. The bitch should be on the lead. The stud dog is brought in, also on the lead, and the two dogs meet, with a little controlled flirting!

**7** The stud dog owner will check your bitch, and may put some petroleum jelly around her vulva. Both dogs should be let off the lead to get to know each other and have a run around to settle them down. However, a very experienced stud dog may be eager to mate immediately.

**8** You will be asked to hold the bitch steady, with her collar. The stud dog owner will support the bitch so that she does not pull away at the vital moment. The dog will mount the bitch and push his penis into the vulva whilst holding his front paws around her waist. The stud dog owner may gently hold the bitch's vulva to check that the dog is going in the correct direction.

**9** It is the second ejaculation of the dog within one minute of penetration that contains the sperm. Then, if the dog is in the correct position, he will start to make thrusting movements. The third part of this process consists of the ejaculation of lots of fluid intermittently and this transports the sperm.

**10** The 'tie' follows, during which the dog's swollen bulbous penis remains inside the bitch's vagina, and the dog and bitch are held physically together. The time of the tie varies with each dog. The times are usually from five minutes to one hour.

**11** At this stage, the stud dog owner turns the dog carefully so he is not resting on the bitch and his four feet are on the floor. He may be standing back to back with the bitch or along her side but they are still physically held together.

**12** Usually the stud dog owner will continue to hold the two dogs, so that the bitch cannot hurt the dog by dragging him.

**13** The tie will break suddenly and the two dogs will part. Sometimes there is quite a lot of prostatic fluid around, but don't worry about this as it does not contain any sperm.

**Note:** the bitch can still conceive and have puppies even if no tie takes place,

### UNSUCCESSFUL MATING

If it hasn't been a 'text book' mating, you may arrange to return and have another mating, but this must not be later than forty-eight hours from the first mating. Most stud dog owners offer a repeat mating if the bitch fails to produce puppies. If the stud dog is young and unproven, not having produced a litter yet, you might pay a stud fee when the bitch has puppies. Some stud dog owners will ask for their choice of puppy instead of the stud fee, but this can lead to problems and it is better to pay the stud fee.

so long as the dog's penis has been inside her for one minute and the dog has ejaculated sperm inside her.

**14** After the mating, the stud dog will be taken away and you can put your bitch back in the car. You must pay the stud fee to the stud dog's owner. Note that the fee is payable for the act that the dog has performed, not for the result, i.e. puppies. You will be given a green form with the dog's particulars which, when you come to register the puppies, must be sent to the Kennel Club. The form is your receipt so be sure to get it on the day of mating. You should already have received a copy of the dog's pedigree and his eye certificate (if a Golden Retriever) and hip-score sheet. If not, that will be given to you now.

## PREGNANCY

The length of pregnancy is usually between sixty and sixty-three days from the day of mating, but it can range from fifty-seven to seventy-two days.

■ You do not need to change your bitch's diet during the first four weeks after the mating. On the twentieth or twenty-first day after mating, the embryo begins to change shape and attach itself to the wall of the uterine horns.

■ The next fourteen days are very important to the growing litter which, at this stage, are still very fragile and susceptible to anything that happens to the bitch, i.e. infections, live vaccination, accidents etc. So during this time be careful and do not expose your bitch to any unnecessary dangers.

### Is your bitch in whelp?

Between twenty and thirty days after mating, it is possible to feel the tiny marble-sized foetuses in the uterus like a row of heads. If it is your bitch's first litter, her teats may become enlarged and bright pink. Another sign of pregnancy is that your bitch's behaviour may change. She may become very careful about her own safety and wellbeing, and may even refuse to allow you out of her sight.

You can have your bitch scanned electronically. This will tell you how many puppies she is expecting (although the number detected by a scan can be inaccurate) or whether she is not in whelp at all. The most obvious physical sign is the enlargement of the stomach, which begins with a slight filling out in the flanks and steadily progresses.

### At the end of the pregnancy

■ The uterine horns become full and cannot continue to lie parallel, so they fold back and drop lower into the abdomen which, again, changes the bitch's figure.

■ The mammary glands enlarge from about the thirty-fifth day onwards, and there will be a discharge of clear or white mucus from the vagina.

■ If at any stage there is a dark bloody or green discharge, you should contact your vet immediately.

### Feeding during pregnancy

During this time, your usual feeding programme for the bitch will change.

■ At the fifth week, add a little extra food and start dividing the food into two meals a day.

■ By the sixth week, she will need twenty-five per cent more food than usual.

■ By the seventh week, a thirty per cent increase is needed, and during the eighth week she will need an extra forty per cent. **Note:** if extra food is not given, your bitch will draw on her own body reserves.

■ The extra food should be protein. When the bitch is seven weeks in whelp, you can divide her food into three meals a day. Check the additives in any complete or commercially prepared foods before giving your bitch supplements. If you are unsure, consult your vet and ask his advice.

## Exercise

The bitch should continue to take her normal exercise throughout most of the pregnancy but she should be discouraged from running excessively, jumping and

### WORMING

Check with your vet before worming your bitch during pregancy. Modern wormers can be obtained from your vet and are very safe to use, so work out a programme with your vet.

any rough play. She needs just enough exercise as is essential to keep her bowels regular and her circulation healthy. A good level of physical fitness is the greatest aid for whelping.

*Like all dogs, even pregnant bitches need daily exercise to stay healthy.*

# Preparing for whelping

## ■ Heating

The room that you have allocated for the whelping must be heated with a constant heat. If somebody offers to lend you a heat lamp, remember that it is better to hang it in the corner for the puppies' benefit rather than too low over the bitch which will make her unsettled. The lamp must be high enough for your bitch to be able to stand up without touching it.

## ■ Whelping box

If you plan to breed more than one litter, you can buy or make your own whelping box. This should be large enough for your bitch to be able to stretch out. Ideally, the sides should be 120 cm² (4 ft²) and the back should be over 60 cm (2 ft) high. The front should be made in removable sections, which can be taken out or put back as required. It is a good idea in the early stages to have a rail around the inside of the box. This helps prevent the bitch

### EQUIPMENT

Be prepared and get all the equipment ready for whelping well in advance of the due date. You will need the following items:
- A hot water bottle
- Some old towelling
- Some vet bed (or polyester fabric) cut into three pieces to fit the whelping box
- A pair of sharp scissors
- A thermometer
- Some suitable disinfectant

**Note:** during the last week of pregnancy, you should wash the bitch's teats regularly with warm water.

accidentally lying on her puppies. It can be removed after the first three to five days.

However, if you are planning on having only one litter, a whelping box can seem an unnecessary expense. You can substitute a large cardboard box (the sort in which refrigerators and large electrical items are packed). Cut the box to shape.

## ■ Urination

During the last couple of weeks of her pregnancy, the bitch may be very heavy and she might need to urinate more frequently. She may even need to be let out in the middle of the night.

## ■ Informing the vet

It is a good idea to let your vet know the expected date for your bitch to start whelping, just in case you need his help or advice when the time comes.

# WHELPING

## The first stage

Retrievers are usually easy whelpers and make good mothers. This first stage varies in time and may be as long as forty-eight hours, although the average is between six and twenty hours. During this stage, the bitch is preparing for the birth and you will recognise the signs (see below). You need to be within sight of your bitch to give her confidence, but do not interfere with her or fuss unnecessarily.

■ **Signs of the first stage**

These include restlessness, panting, digging up her bed and refusing food. Keep an eye on her as you don't want her to dig a hole outside ready for whelping! However, this digging behaviour is part of the normal cycle. Often, during this stage of whelping, a bitch gets a far-away look in her eyes.

■ **The bitch's temperature**

One of the best ways of ascertaining when whelping will commence is to take the bitch's temperature. The most reliable guide is a drop in her temperature. In the last weeks of pregnancy, the temperature is on average 37.7°C (100°F). However, at the onset of whelping, the temperature drops to 37°C (97.9°F). It may stay at this level for only a few hours, so you will have to take the bitch's temperature twice a day for about three days before whelping for a guide, and then record the readings on a chart. Labour should start within twenty-four hours of the lowest temperature (37°C) being marked down. **Note:** as the signs become more vigorous and less intermittent, the bitch should progress on to stage two. However, if you feel that things are not progressing and that time is passing by without much happening, then telephone your vet. It might be the first stages of uterine inertia and your vet will know what to do.

## The second stage

Throughout her pregnancy, your bitch will probably have a little mucoid discharge from the vulva and this will now increase in volume.

■ In the first stage, the birth passage (cervix) softens and dilates so that the puppies pass from the uterus down the vagina and out.

■ In the second stage, the cervix is fully dilated and now you see a gentle ripple, then a push as the bitch pushes down in contractions. Watch carefully as these contractions can be almost imperceptible at first.

■ Make a note of the time when the contractions start. If the bitch has been straining for two hours and no puppy has appeared, you should consult your vet.

■ The next thing that happens is the appearance at the vulva of a black fluid bag. This membrane has been around each puppy during gestation and is now helping to lubricate it out. Sometimes this water bag bursts inside the bitch and then the contents gush out. The bag does not contain a puppy but there should be one not far behind.

■ The bitch may stand, sit or lie down to have her puppies – it does not matter which method she chooses. However, if she is standing, you must be ready to catch the emerging puppies.

■ The puppy should slide out quickly. It is inside a thin bag of membrane, which has its own placenta or afterbirth attached to the umbilical cord. Puppies are usually born head first, but they can often be hind feet first. There are also breech births, in which a puppy is presented rump first, with the hind legs tucked under the body.

■ The bitch will usually break the bag, freeing the puppy, and she will cut through the umbilical cord with her teeth. She will eat the placenta (this is good for her, and, in the wild, this would be her food supply) and she will then set about resuscitating the puppy, usually quite roughly. Don't worry – the licking gets the puppy's lungs inflated and the blood supply moving.

■ All this is done very quickly, but if the bitch does not seem to know what to do, then you will have to do it for her. With the tip of your finger, gently remove the membrane around the puppy's mouth to enable it to breathe. Cut the umbilical cord with some sharp disinfected scissors, about 5-7.5 cm (2-3 in) from the puppy. Rub the puppy with a towel to dry it, then give it to the bitch who will lick it. You should then put the puppy on to a teat to feed.

## CAESAREAN BIRTHS

Sometimes a bitch has to have a Caesarean and you will need your vet's advice on this. If some puppies have been born naturally, leave them in a box on a hot water bottle covered with a towel – they will come to no harm without food for a few hours. Do not at this stage think that they need something to drink and give them a puppy feeder; this will do more harm than good.

Modern anaesthetics mean that the bitch will recover quickly after a Caesarean. When you bring her back into the whelping box, make her comfortable. Bring the puppies in and smear a little of her vaginal discharge over them; this helps her to start licking them. Stay with them until they are all suckling and the bitch is obviously mothering them.

■ The interval between puppies being born varies in time, but usually the bitch will have two or three puppies at short intervals of ten to thirty minutes, followed by a rest of one to two hours before starting again.

**Note:** if the bitch strains and no puppies arrive after two hours, you should get in touch with your vet.

■ Some breeders place a warm hot water bottle covered by a towel in a box next to the bitch while she is whelping. When her puppies are born they can be put in the box to keep warm, and then, when the birth process is over, back they go on to the teats. But generally the bitch is happier cleaning and nursing the puppies between births and will keep the whelping area clean.

## Whelping tips

■ During the whelping, check the number of afterbirths expelled and write it down. If you know of any that have been retained, telephone your vet and ask for advice.

■ Throughout the whelping, offer your bitch drinks of milk and glucose. If the whelping is very long and your bitch appears tired, add a teaspoon of brandy but do not give her any food.

## When is the whelping over?

After the whelping, your bitch may go to sleep – most bitches relax afterwards.

You should arrange for your vet to call to see the bitch the following day in order to check that the uterus is empty and that there is no sign of infection. For about twenty-four hours after whelping the bitch will have a greenish discharge, followed by a brownish-red one which gradually lessens over several weeks.

**Note:** if she has a foul-smelling black discharge, contact your vet immediately.

*Young puppies are fed by their mother and weaning should not start until three weeks old.*

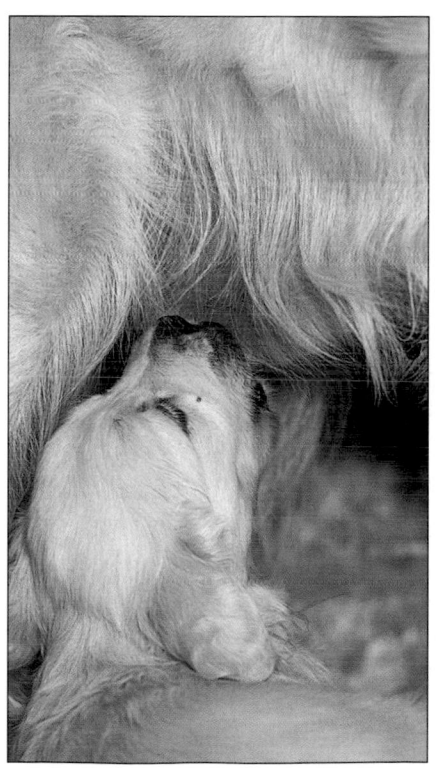

# POSTNATAL CARE

## Postnatal care

■ It is always important that puppies are kept warm, especially in the first critical thirty-six hours of their lives. A new-born puppy's body temperature is low compared with that of an adult, so use the heat lamp as required.

■ The bitch needs peace and quiet, especially while the puppies are still very young so do not allow any visitors yet. During the first few days, you will have to take your bitch out to relieve herself, probably on a lead as she will not want to leave her puppies.

■ After all that both you and your bitch have gone through, neither of you will want to lose any puppies, so for the first twenty-four hours it is a good idea not to leave her just in case she lies on any puppies in the night.

## Feeding the bitch

The bitch should be fed a light diet for the first twenty-four hours: scrambled eggs, fish, chicken, milk and plenty of clean water. Initially, you will need to feed her in the whelping box. She will need the best-quality food to help make the best-quality milk. After twenty-four hours, she can return to her normal diet, but follow the manufacturer's instructions regarding the amounts for nursing bitches if you use a complete food.

For other ways of feeding, check that the food is rich in protein, and increase the amount gradually until the bitch is eating about three times her maintenance diet. Feed her daily allowance as three separate meals. If you give her chicken or tripe, calcium and vitamin supplements must be used.

## Feeding the puppies

Check that all the puppies are suckling well and are getting sufficient milk. If the litter is large and some puppies are falling behind, you can top them up with special milk supplements which are available from your vet or local pet store. You will need a puppy feeder and must be very careful when feeding them as you can cause a puppy to choke if you are not careful.

If the litter is small, check that the bitch's teats do not become too full and hard, which can lead to mastitis. Hold a warm cloth gently on the area and then express the milk.

## The bitch and her puppies

Bitches vary in how long they will stay all the time with their puppies. After the first three to four days, they will start to stay out of the box for longer periods. At the end of the first week, gently cut the tips of the puppies' nails with a pair of scissors to prevent them hurting the bitch, and then cut them once a week thereafter until they go to their new homes.

Never leave the bitch in the box with her puppies once they start really moving around unless she can get away from them easily. The front of the whelping box should be of a height that she can step over it yet the puppies cannot climb out. Bitches will often lie outside the box with their heads over the side, seeing that all is well within, and when it is feeding time for the puppies they pop back into the box.

## Weaning

■  You can start weaning the puppies, depending on the size of the litter, from about three weeks of age. If the bitch is feeding them very well, they may be slow to wean. But before you wean them, they must be wormed. Use a liquid wormer which can be obtained from the vet. Worm the puppies at three, five and seven weeks.

■  It is better to start the puppies off on solids rather than giving them milk to lap

*These puppies are lined up ready for a drink from their mother. Her milk contains all the nutrients they need.*

while they are still being fed by their mother. You can start by feeding them small scraps of meat and puppy meal or a complete specially formulated puppy food which you can buy from your pet shop.

■ If you feed meat and puppy meal plus additives when starting to wean, give the puppies top-quality raw steak mince, about 25 g (1 oz) per puppy. Make sure that you don't feed the same puppy twice! Offer each puppy one meal a day for four days, and then another meal so that it is fed morning and night, with its mother's milk the rest of the time.

■ At four to five weeks, start the puppies lapping with some prepared puppy milk and cereal plus honey in a small saucer. It should be of a gruel-like consistency, not too thin. After feeding,

wipe the puppies' faces and paws with a damp cloth.

■ When you start weaning the puppies, you can begin to reduce the amount of food you are feeding the bitch. By the time that the puppies are weaned, she should be back on her normal diet.

## Feeding older puppies

■ By the time they are eight weeks old, the puppies should be eating four meals a day. If they are on a complete feed, follow the directions on the can or packet; otherwise, feed them 420 g (14 oz) meat, 550 ml (1 pint) specially formulated milk and 50 g (2 oz) puppy meal or mixer. At ten to twelve weeks, fresh goat's or cow's milk can be given.

■ Between four and five months, reduce

---

### FEEDING GUIDELINES

■ At five weeks, the puppies should be on five meals a day. If they are on a diet of a complete food, you should follow the instructions. If you are feeding fresh food, here are some feeding guidelines:
8:00am - meat
10:30am - milk
1:30pm - milk and cereal
5:30pm - meat
9:30pm - milk and cereal plus additives, but follow the directions carefully as too much is as dangerous as too little.

■ At four weeks, feed them 75 g (3 oz) of meat at each feed plus milk.

■ At five weeks, feed them 115 g (4 oz) of meat at each feed plus 550 ml (1 pint) of milk daily.

■ At six weeks, feed them 150 g (5 oz) of meat at each feed plus 550 ml (1 pint) of milk daily. You can start adding some puppy meal or small bite mixer also at this stage of the puppies' development. Make sure that it is well soaked.

■ At seven weeks, feed them 175 g (6 oz) of meat at each feed plus 550 ml (1 pint) of milk daily.

■ At eight weeks, feed them 200 g (7 oz) of meat daily plus milk.

## MOTHER AND PUPS

Puppies are usually completely weaned by the time they are six weeks old, although for the bitch's comfort they might still be having a drink from her at night. From when the puppies are three to four weeks, the bitch will probably have just gone in to feed and sleep with them and play with them. As they get bigger, the bitch will usually just dash in quickly to feed the puppies and then dash out again. Even when her milk has dried up, she will still enjoy visiting the pups and playing with them. This is when they start to learn from their mother the behaviour within the pack. The puppies should not leave the litter and go to their new homes before they are seven or eight weeks old.

the number of feeds to three daily with increased amounts of food at each meal. At six months, you can cut them down to two meals, while at nine months they will require only one meal. However, if you wish, you can keep your dog on two meals. By the age of nine months, the main growing cycle has been completed.

### Finding homes for the puppies

It is important to find suitable owners for the puppies and you should take care to sell them only to people who will give them good homes. You should ask potential owners about their lifestyle, their house and garden and whether a Retriever puppy will be a suitable pet for them.

Tell the new owners that you are there to help them if they have any problems with the puppy. Also, if through unforeseen circumstances they cannot keep the dog, you should be told so that you can help with rehoming. Make sure that you give the new owners a diet sheet so that they feed the puppy correctly.

*A bottle feeder can be used sometimes to top up puppies in large litters who may not get enough milk.*

# CHAPTER SEVEN

# SHOWING YOUR DOG

## DOG SHOWS

Like most pet owners, you probably never considered showing your puppy or dog – all you wanted was a dog who would become a much-loved member of your family, a healthy, good representative of the breed with the character that first attracted you to owning a Retriever.

### Types of dog shows

All the dog shows in the UK are licensed by the Kennel Club. They are usually run by a canine or breed society.

■ **Primary Shows**

Entry is limited to members of the Show Society and there are classes for puppies and novice dogs. No big winners at Championship Shows or Challenge Certificate winners are permitted.

■ **Limited and Sanction Shows**

Entry is limited to members of the Show Society. No winners of Challenge Certificates can be shown.

■ **Open Shows**

These shows are open to all exhibitors. Champions and Challenge Certificate winners can compete but no Challenge Certificates can be offered. Breed clubs can also have an Open Show for one breed.

■ **Championship Shows**

These are open to all scheduled breeds, and Kennel Club Challenge Certificates are offered. Three such Challenge Certificates awarded by three different judges allow a Retriever to be called a 'Show Champion'. However, one of the Challenge Certificates must be won when the dog is over twelve months old.

■ **Exemption Shows**

These are often run in conjunction with charity events. There are some classes for pedigree dogs.

### Choosing and finding a show

How do you find out when and where the shows are being held and how to go about entering them? You can contact the Kennel Club (see page 144) and tell them which breed you own and where you live. They will give you details of your nearest breed club.

The Secretary of the club can supply information on shows in your area, and can advise whether there is somebody who lives near you who could help with presentation for the showring with your puppy.

## Ringcraft classes

Another method of preparing your puppy for showing is to find out if any local ringcraft classes are advertised on the board in your vet's surgery. They are usually run by your local dog society and are an excellent way of learning what to do in the show ring. You cannot show your puppy until he is six months old, but once the vaccination programme has been completed you can take him to a ringcraft class.

Initially, just sit and watch. Don't let your puppy get involved with other dogs – you don't want him to be frightened or to get hurt because somebody cannot control their dog. From the age of four months

*Hans Troedsson and Valerie Foss's home-bred Show Champion Elswood the Highlander is seen here winning the Challenge Certificate at Crufts.*

onwards, your puppy can take part.

You will soon become acquainted with show procedures. Your puppy will get used to being examined by a stranger and you will learn how to stand him still and move him to the best advantage to show off all his good points. Ringcraft is an enjoyable social occasion with none of the competitiveness of a show. People have time to help and schedules of local shows are usually displayed.

## WHAT IS A SCHEDULE?

A schedule is a form with details of the show, its timing and location and closing date for entries – this is important for they must be sent off in time. The closing date for Championship Shows is about six weeks before the show, but Open and Sanction Shows close their entries nearer to the show date.

You will receive an entry form on which you fill in your dog's particulars. You can copy these from your Kennel Club registration form. You must decide which classes to enter at the show and write the numbers of the classes chosen on the entry form; do not be tempted to enter every class.

If your dog is eligible for the age restricted classes, i.e. special puppy, puppy, junior and special yearling, then you can work your way gradually through them. If your dog is still a puppy, just enter in the puppy classes. Shows are very tiring, both mentally and physically, for dogs, especially puppies. So don't overdo it.

## Handling your dog at a show

You handle your dog in the show ring to show off his good points (remember the Standard to which judges mentally compare your dog) and to try to disguise his faults or weaknesses. You have to observe a lot of good handlers before you know what you have to do. This also makes you realise that the perfect dog, construction-wise, has never been born and yours is not the exception.

The judge examines each dog in the class individually, opening the mouth to check for correct dentition, feeling the spring of the rib, the length of tail and the coat texture. Then he will ask the handler to 'Move your dog, please', and this is usually performed in a triangle so that the judge can see the dog's rear and profile movement to check on his toplines, and then the front movement as the dog comes back to him. Moving means getting your dog to trot freely at your side, neither pulling nor being dragged. This takes quite a lot of practice until he does it perfectly. Retrievers can be shown in two ways: free standing or set up (stacked).

■ **Free standing:** you walk your dog into position, with the feet in the correct place and tail gently wagging. You need some of your dog's favourite titbits so that he keeps the pose looking at your pocket. He knows that after a little wait, he will get a reward.

■ **Set up (stacked):** you keep your hand under the dog's chin, place the front feet and then the hind feet into position so that the dog is standing correctly and then hold the end of the tail out in a straight line, continuing the line of the topline.

Both methods are used whilst the judge is looking at the dog. Both look good when done correctly, but they need practice at home and at ringcraft classes before you go to shows. Never allow your puppy or adult to get bored – about five minutes' practice a day is sufficient. Use a command word, such as 'Stand' or 'Stay', which your dog associates with what you want. Place his feet, then say the chosen word and his name. Hold the position at the beginning for a minute or two, giving your dog lots of praise and, at the end, a titbit.

Never try the moving session until your dog has been exercised. Start off by walking quickly, saying 'Heel' and then the dog's name. This is work so don't allow him to sniff the ground. Plan out how far you want to move, then turn and return to your starting position. When you come back and stop, make your dog stand and pose for a second. This will give the judge a final glance after your individual show. Again, you should practise this for about five minutes a day but always let your dog have a run beforehand.

*The judge will walk around, looking at all the dogs being shown in a class before making his decision.*

## GROOMING FOR SHOWING

If you have fed and exercised your dog correctly, he should be in good condition. Now it's a case of tidying, grooming and trimming him. Golden, Curly Coat and Flat Coat Retrievers are all different and you should follow the instructions for your breed.

### Golden Retrievers

The best way to start trimming is to watch somebody who has considerable expertise, perhaps the breeder of your

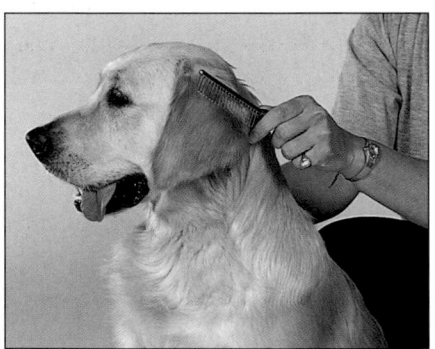

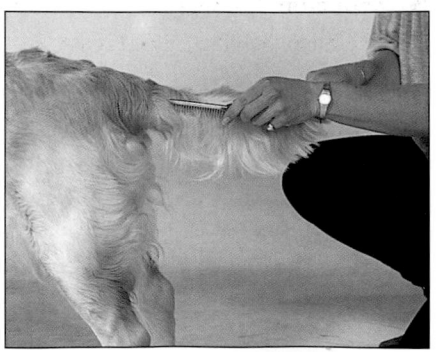

puppy. Some breed clubs hold seminars at which experts demonstrate how to trim a show dog correctly.

### Grooming a puppy

Right from the beginning, you should have accustomed your puppy to being groomed with five minutes' gentle brushing every day. This will help him to

*Show dogs must be groomed and trimmed carefully to prepare them for showing. A metal comb is used to gently comb through the hair on the head and ears, body, legs, feet and tail, teasing out any tangles. You can train the dog from puppyhood to stand still while you do this and to enjoy the experience.*

## TRIMMING EQUIPMENT

The following items are suitable for all three breeds of Retrievers.
- Thinning scissors (with serrated edges)
- Straight-edged scissors
- Nail cutters – the guillotine type are easy to use
- A metal comb with not too much width between the teeth
- A metal comb with very fine teeth
- A bristle brush
- A hound glove – after grooming with the special wire side, do a final polish with the cloth side
- A magnet stripping knife

learn to stand still. If you have an old table which is large enough for the dog to stand on comfortably, cover it with a sheet of ridged rubber to prevent him slipping. It is easier to trim him when he is level with you.

## Trimming for showing

- If your dog is an adult with a lot of coat, don't start the night before the show. Begin preparing him two to three weeks beforehand for about one hour each week. Then give him a final tidy up the night before the show.
- Remember that it is better to remove too little hair than to trim too much the first time.
- Use thinning scissors and then comb

through the dog's coat to see what you have removed.

## The first session

Start off by trimming the dog's chest, underneath the ears and also the hair on top of and around the ear flap; be careful under the ear as there is a double fold. Trim around the edges of the ear with the straight scissors. Check that the neck trimming runs into the shoulder trimming and it looks as one.

### ■ Trimming the tail

Hold the tail out; you want to end up with longer hair at the base which becomes progressively shorter until it rounds off at the tip. Take your straight scissors and trim from the tip to the root in an arc. The hair at its longest point should be about 12.5 cm (5 in). Comb and check.

### ■ Tidying the hair

Tidy any long hair that does not lie flat by pulling against the magnet stripper; this stripper can also be used on top of the dog's ears.

### ■ Trimming the feet

This is best done with the dog lying

## TRIMMING TIPS

- Never cut across the hair.
- Use an upward movement with the scissors underneath the top layer.
- Keep combing after each scissor movement.

down. You pull the excess long hair up between the toes and cut down with the straight scissors. Trim under the foot around the pads, removing any excess fur. Tidy the excess hair from the hock to the foot with the thinning scissors.

■ **Cutting the nails**

Be careful not to cut the quick of each nail – guillotine-type cutters are good for this. If the nails are light in colour you can see the quick but you must take care with dark nails.

■ **Washing your dog**

Bath your dog about three days before the show; this gives the coat a chance to get back its natural gloss. Use a good-quality dog shampoo and finish off with a cream rinse specifically designed for dogs. Rinse all the soap out thoroughly.

Towel your dog well to remove as much water as possible, then either dry him with a hair dryer, combing all the time, or comb dry. Do not let him lie down and go to sleep until he is dry, or the coat will dry rough with the hair sticking up. **Note:** it is important to let the dog's coat dry flat. You can do this by constant combing or by using a hair dryer and combing at the same time.

## Flat Coated Retrievers

They need less trimming than Golden Retrievers, but they must be tidy.

**1** Comb the coat to remove any dead hair.

**2** Gently remove the fluffy hair on top of each ear flap with thinning scissors or a magnet stripping knife. Tidy under the ears so they lie flat against the head.

**3** Trim the feet by pulling up the excess long hair between the toes and cutting down with the straight scissors. Trim under the foot around the pads, removing any excess fur. Tidy the excess hair (comb it out first to see how much the dog has) from hock to foot with the thinning scissors.

■ **Trimming the tail**

As with a Golden Retriever, you want to end up with longer hair at the base of the tail becoming gradually shorter until it rounds off at the tip. With your straight scissors, trim from the tip to the root in an arc. The hair at its longest point should be about 12.5 cm (5 in). Comb.

■ **Preparing the coat**

Never wash your dog within three days of a show – it will make the coat fluffy. He does not need the show washing a Golden Retriever requires. The coat must be shiny and this will not happen with too much water.

## Curly Coat Retrievers

These dogs are different from the other Retrievers. You will need the following grooming equipment: straight scissors, thinning scissors, a sponge and a comb with wide teeth.

■ **Trimming the ears**

With the straight scissors, trim along the

edge of each ear and then tidy the curls to make them short. Using the thinning scissors, trim the coat underneath the ears, giving a smooth line to the top of the head.

■ **Trimming the neck and body**
Tidy the dog's throat and neck down to the chest with the straight scissors. Trim the curls on the body to make him look neat but don't cut them too short.

■ **Trimming the hocks and tail**
Cut the hair short on the hocks. Tidy and trim around the tip of the tail, then cut the hair on the underside. Trim the curls on the rest of the tail, taking care not to make them too short.

■ **Trimming the feet**
To trim any untidy hair between the toes, pull the hair upwards and cut it downwards. Keep the dog's nails tidy.

■ **Washing your dog**
Keeping your dog's coat in top show

*Curly Coated Retrievers must be prepared for showing by wetting the coat thoroughly every day – you can use a wet sponge or a spray filled with water. Use a metal comb to gently comb through the curls, massaging the coat with your fingertips. Do not use shampoo on your dog's coat.*

condition means that it should be wetted thoroughly once a day. For a pet dog who is not being shown, once a fortnight is enough. A swim every day would be ideal. Otherwise, you should really soak the coat with water (no shampoo), using a sponge. Massage the coat all over with your fingertips.

### CASTING TIP

When your dog is casting his coat, comb it well to remove any dead coat, using a wide-toothed comb.

## AT THE SHOW

Most people start off by entering their dog at a breed club's Open Show. If you are showing a puppy, he should be in good condition with a gleaming coat.

■ Take a bag with you containing grooming equipment, water and a bowl. If it is not a benched show you will need a blanket for your dog to lie on. If he is a Curly Coated Retriever, you will also need a spray filled with water to spray on him before you go in the ring.

■ As well as his normal collar and lead, your dog will need a show lead in the ring. There are many different types and colours. A good option is a long leather one with a ring in the end which serves as both collar and lead.

■ If you have trained your dog to show on food bait, take some in a plastic bag. You can buy dog snacks in your pet shop or cook some liver until it is hard, almost like rubber.

■ Pack a 'poop bag' to remove any mess your dog might make whilst he is exercising around the show ground.

### Time of arrival

If your puppy is entered in the first class of the show, you should aim to arrive an hour before the class is scheduled to start. You need to allow time to exercise

your puppy when you first get there. You will also have to groom him and have a quick practice session for what is to come. After that, you are in at the deep end. You are going to enjoy this experience and your dog will too.

### Showing your puppy

When you enter the ring, you will be given your dog's number to wear. Pin it on with a ring clip or a safety pin. It is best not to stand first; let some other people go before you and watch what they do. However, don't go last, as your puppy may get bored awaiting his turn.

When it's your turn, stand your puppy as you have been practising. The judge will then:

1 Stand and just look at your dog.

2 Approach the dog from the front.

3 Carefully go over each point he/she wishes to examine using the hands.

4 Open the mouth to see the correct dentition. If your dog is not very happy about this, you should gently practise doing it yourself once a day until he grows accustomed to it. Do it quickly and quietly for thirty seconds only.

5 Replace the dog's front, to check that it is correct, feel the ribs and shoulders and check the texture of the coat.

6 Check that the tail is the correct length,

## SHOWING ADVICE

■ Start at the smaller shows before progressing to the Championship Shows. General Championship Shows (all breeds) are benched, i.e. there is a wooden 'seat' for the dog between two metal pieces with metal at the back. The dogs must be tied to the bench with a benching chain fixed to their collars – never to a choke chain which could cause them to be strangled.

■ For at least the first four shows you enter, your dog must not be left alone on the bench. Gradually you can increase the time you leave him alone, starting with ten minutes and progressing to thirty or forty-five minutes. He must be taken off the bench for exercise and showing.

■ You will need a piece of bedding to go on the bench. Some breed Championship Shows are unbenched and it is a much more friendly way to take part at a show.

and the dog is in good muscular condition.

**7** Ask you to move in a triangle from corner to corner across the ring and back again to observe the dog's profile movement and topline. All the class may be requested to do this, first in a circular movement, then straight up and down to see the front and rear movement when you are examined individually.

**8** Finally, you should stand still for a minute while the judge has a last look before going back into the line.

**9** When the judge has individually examined each dog in the class, stand your dog ready. The judge will walk along the line, then stand back and, if it is a large class, make a shortlist. If your dog is called out, stay calm and set him up, keeping him interested. You will be asked for a final movement up and down, and then the judge will make his decision. If you have been chosen, line up where the steward tells you. Whether you have come first or were not even shortlisted, keep on trying.

# PART THREE

# HEALTHCARE

In this section on healthcare, there is expert
practical advice on how to keep your dog fit and
healthy and how to prevent many common health
problems which beset dogs, together with
information on infectious canine illnesses and
other medical conditions and diseases and the
special health problems that may affect Retrievers
as a breed, especially inherited ones such as hip
dysplasia. Essential first-aid techniques for use in
a wide range of common accidents and
emergencies, including road accidents and dog
fights, are also featured, with easy-to-follow step-
by-step illustrated guides and advice on what
you can do yourself and when you should
seek expert veterinary help.

# HEALTH MAINTENANCE

Throughout the health section of this book, where comments relate equally to the dog or the bitch, we have used the term 'he' to avoid the repeated, clumsy use of 'he or she'.

## SIGNS OF A HEALTHY DOG

### ■ Appearance and behaviour
In general, a healthy dog looks healthy. He wants to play with you, as games are a very important part of a dog's life. A Retriever, being developed as a working gun dog, should always be ready for his walk, and will require a lot of exercise.

### ■ Eyes and nose
His eyes are bright and alert, and, apart from the small amount of 'sleep' in the inner corners, there is no discharge. His nose is usually cold and wet with no discharge, although a little clear fluid can be normal.

### ■ Ears
His ears are also alert and very responsive to sounds around him. In the Retriever, the ears are normally folded forwards obscuring the ear opening. The inside of his ear flap is pale pink in appearance and silky in texture. No wax will be visible and there will be no unpleasant smell. He will not scratch his ears much, or shake his head excessively.

### ■ Coat
A healthy Retriever's coat will be glossy and feel pleasant to the touch. He will not scratch excessively and scurf will be not be present.

His coat will smell 'doggy' but not unpleasant, and he will probably continuously shed hairs (moult) to some degree, especially if he lives indoors with the family.

### ■ Teeth
The teeth of a healthy dog should be white and smooth. If they are yellow and dull there may be plaque or tartar formation.

### ■ Claws
A dog's claws should not be broken or too long. There is a short non-sensitive tip, as in our nails. The claw should end at the ground, level with the pad. Dogs will not pay much attention to their feet, apart from normal washing, but excessive licking can indicate disease. Retrievers have five toes on the front feet, with one in our 'thumb' position called the dew claw, and four on the hind feet. If a puppy is born with a dew claw on a hind foot, it is usually removed at three to five days of age as they become pendulous and are often injured as an adult.

### ■ Stools
A healthy dog will pass stools between once and six times a day depending on diet, temperament and opportunity.

### ■ Urination
A male dog will urinate numerous times on a walk as this is territorial behaviour. Bitches usually urinate less often.

### ■ Weight
A healthy dog will look in good bodily condition for his size: not too fat and not too

## POINTS OF THE RETRIEVER

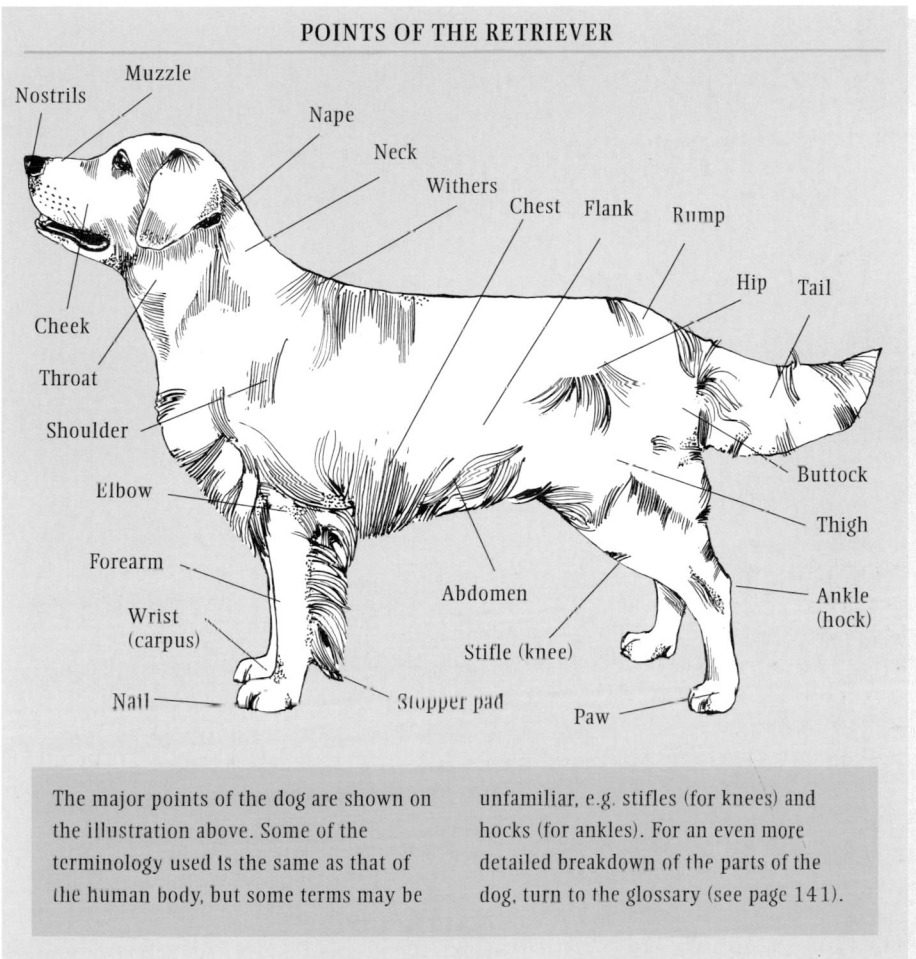

The major points of the dog are shown on the illustration above. Some of the terminology used is the same as that of the human body, but some terms may be unfamiliar, e.g. stifles (for knees) and hocks (for ankles). For an even more detailed breakdown of the parts of the dog, turn to the glossary (see page 141).

thin. Sixty per cent of dogs nowadays are overweight, so you should try to balance the diet of your Retriever with the right amount of exercise.

### ■ Feeding

Your dog will usually be ready for his meal and once adult, he should be fed regularly at the same time each day. Most dogs require one meal a day, but some healthy dogs seem to require two meals daily just to maintain a normal weight. These are the very active dogs who tend to 'burn off' more calories.

## DIET

### ■ Feeding a puppy

The correct diet as a pup is essential to allow him to achieve his full potential during the growing phase. In a Retriever this is up to eighteen months to two years of age. Many

## EXAMINING YOUR DOG

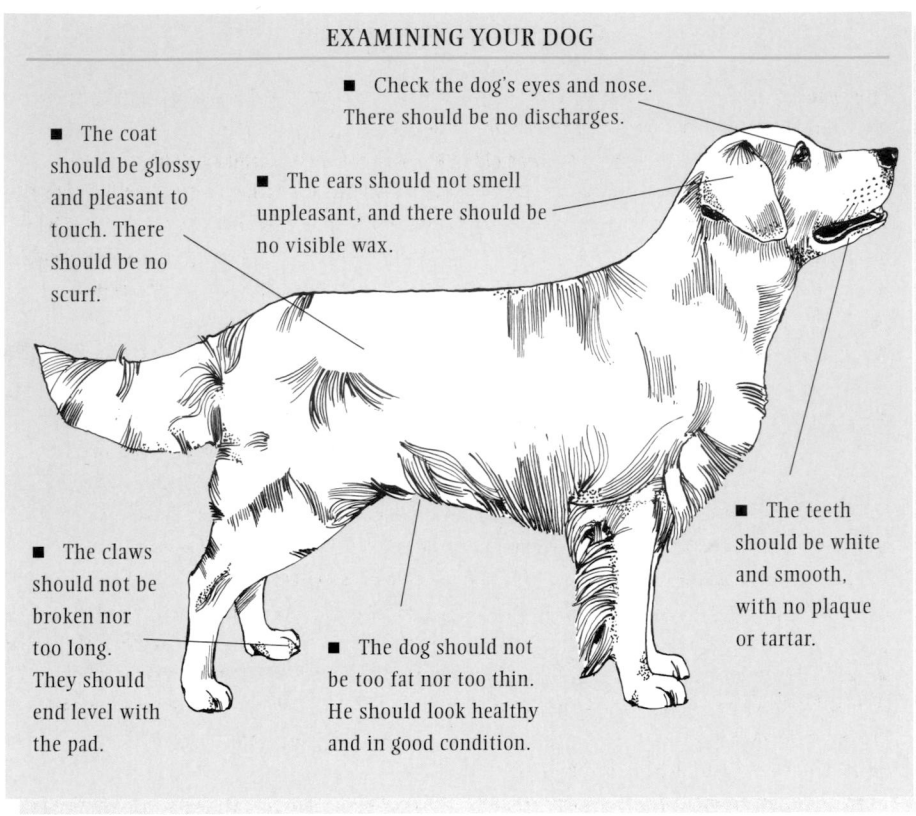

- Check the dog's eyes and nose. There should be no discharges.

- The coat should be glossy and pleasant to touch. There should be no scurf.

- The ears should not smell unpleasant, and there should be no visible wax.

- The teeth should be white and smooth, with no plaque or tartar.

- The claws should not be broken nor too long. They should end level with the pad.

- The dog should not be too fat nor too thin. He should look healthy and in good condition.

home-made diets are deficient in various ingredients just because owners do not fully appreciate the balance that is required. It is far better to rely on one of the correctly formulated and prepared commercial diets which will contain the correct amounts and proportions of essential nutrients, such as protein, carbohydrates, fats, roughage, minerals, such as calcium and phosphorus, and essential vitamins.

Modern thinking is that the complete, dried, extruded diets available now have so many advantages that the new puppy could be put on to a 'growth' formula diet of this type from as early as four weeks. Crunchy diets such as these have advantages in dental care also. However,

there are some excellent canned and semi-moist diets available but care should be taken to check whether these are complete diets, or complementary foods which require biscuits and other ingredients to be added. If you really know your diets, it is of course possible to formulate a home-prepared diet from fresh ingredients.

A puppy should be fed four times a day until he is three months of age, and with a complete dried food this can be left down so that he can help himself to food whenever he feels hungry. The exact amount of food will depend on his age and the type of food, and if instructions are not included on the packet, you should consult your vet.

## CARE OF THE OLDER DOG

Provided that he has been well cared for throughout his life, there may be no need to treat the older Retriever any differently as old age approaches. However, Retrievers seem particularly prone to obesity in old age.

■ **Diet**

This should be chosen to:

■ Improve existing problems

■ Slow or prevent the development of disease

■ Enable the dog to maintain his ideal body weight

■ Be highly palatable and digestible

■ Contain an increased amount of fatty acids, vitamins (especially A, B and E) and certain minerals, notably zinc

■ Contain reduced amounts of protein, phosphorus and sodium

■ **Fitness and exercise**

A healthy Retriever should hardly need to reduce his exercise until he is over ten years old. There should be no sudden change in routine; a sudden increase in exercise is as wrong as a sudden drop. Let the dog tell you when he has had enough. If he lags behind, has difficulty in walking, breathing, or getting to his feet after a long walk, then it is time to consider a health check. As dogs age, they need a good diet, company, comfort, and a change of scenery to add interest to their lives.

■ **Avoiding obesity**

■ As the body ages, all body systems age with it. The heart and circulation, lungs, muscles and joints are not as efficient. These should all be able to support and transport a dog of the correct weight but may fail if the dog is grossly overweight.

■ A Retriever of normal weight will approach old age with a greater likelihood of reaching it. It is wise to diet your dog at this stage if you have let his weight increase. Food intake can be increased almost to normal when the weight loss has been achieved.

■ Reduce the calorie intake to about sixty per cent of normal, to encourage the conversion of body fat back into energy. Feed a high-fibre diet so that the dog does not feel hungry. Maintenance levels of essential nutrients, such as protein, vitamins and minerals, must be provided so that deficiencies do not occur.

■ Your veterinary surgeon will be able to supply or advise on the choice of several prescription low-calorie diets available in both dried and canned form, or instruct you on how to mix your own

### The dog's lifespan

Most people assume that seven years of our lives are equivalent to one year of a dog's. However, a more accurate comparison would be as follows:

■ 1 dog year = 15 human years

■ 3 dog years = 30 human years

■ 6 dog years = 40 human years

■ 9 dog years = 55 human years

■ 12 dog years = 65 human years

■ 15 dog years = 80 human years

**Note:** this is only an approximate guide as the larger breeds of dog tend not to live as long as the smaller breeds.

At three months of age, he should be fed three times daily, but each meal should have more in it. By six months of age he could be down to two larger meals a day, still of a puppy or growth formula food. He should remain on this type of food until twelve to eighteen months of age, and then change to an adult maintenance version.

■ **Feeding an adult dog**

Adult dogs can be fed on any one of the excellent range of quality dog foods now available. Your vet is the best person to advise you as to the best diet for your Retriever, and this advice will vary depending on his age, amount of exercise, and condition.

■ **Feeding an older dog**

From the age of nine or ten years on, your Retriever may benefit from a change to a diet specially formulated for the older dog, as he will have differing requirements as his body organs age a little. Your vet is the best person to discuss this with, as he will be able to assess his general condition and requirements.

## EXERCISE

## Exercising a puppy

As a puppy, your Retriever should not be given too much exercise as his joints are not fully formed. At the age that you acquire him, usually six to eight weeks of age, he will need gentle, frequent forays into your garden, or other people's gardens provided they are not open to stray dogs. He can and should meet other vaccinated, reliable dogs or puppies and play with them. He will also enjoy energetic games with you, but remember that in any tug-of-war type contest you should win!

■ **Exercise and vaccinations**

Although you should be taking your puppy out with you to accustom him to the sights and sounds of normal life, at this stage you should not put him down on the ground in public places until the vaccination course is completed, because of the risk of infection.

■ **Exercise after vaccinations**

About a week after his second vaccination, you will be able to take him out for walks, but remember that at this stage he is equivalent to a toddler. His bones have not calcified, his joints are still developing, and too much strenuous exercise can affect normal development. This applies especially to large breeds with rapid growth like Retrievers, which at this stage may be gaining up to 2kg (3.6lb) a week. Perhaps three walks daily for about half an hour each is ample by about four months of age, rising to two to three hours by the time he reaches six months. At this stage, as his bones and joints develop, he could then be taken for more vigorous runs in the country. However, he should not be involved in really tiring exercise until nine months to a year old, by which time his joints have almost fully matured, and his bones fully calcified.

## Exercising an adult dog

■ **Exercise after six months**

As an adult dog, his exercise tolerance will be almost limitless, certainly better than most of ours! It is essential that such a lively, active, intelligent breed as the Retriever has an adequate amount of exercise daily – it is not really sufficient to provide exercise just at weekends. A daily quota of one to two hours of interesting, energetic exercise is essential. During exercise they enjoy games such as retrieving and finding hidden objects, so try to exercise his brain as well as his body.

## DAILY CARE

There are several things that you should be carrying out daily for your dog to keep him in first-class condition.

- **Grooming**

All dogs benefit from a daily grooming session. Use a stiff brush or comb obtained from your vet or pet shop, and ensure you specify that it is for a Retriever as brushes vary. Comb or brush in the direction of the lie of the hair. Hair is constantly growing and being shed, especially in dogs that live indoors with us, as their bodies become confused as to which season it is in a uniformly warm house. Brushing removes dead hair and scurf, and stimulates the sebaceous glands to produce the natural oils that keep the coat glossy. Constant moulting seems to be a particular problem of the Retrievers.

- **Bathing**

Dogs should not require frequent baths, but can benefit from a periodic shampoo using a

## GENERAL INSPECTION

A full inspection of your dog is not necessary on a daily basis, unless you notice something different about him. However, it is as well to cast your eyes over him to ensure that:

- The coat and skin are in good order
- The eyes are bright
- The ears are clean
- The dog is not lame

Check that he has eaten his food, and that his stools and urine look normal.

dog shampoo with a conditioner included.

- **Feeding**

Dogs do not benefit from a frequently changed diet; their digestive systems seem to get used to a regular diet. They do not worry if they have the same every day – that is a human trait – so establish a complete nutritious diet that your dog enjoys and stick to it.

## VACCINATIONS

Vaccination is the administration of a modified live, or killed, form of an infection which does not cause illness in the dog, but instead stimulates the formation of antibodies against the disease itself.

There are four major diseases against which all dogs should be vaccinated. These are:

- Canine distemper (also called hardpad)
- Infectious canine hepatitis
- Leptospirosis
- Canine parvovirus

Many vaccination courses now include a component against parainfluenza virus, one

of the causes of kennel cough, that scourge of boarding and breeding kennels. A separate vaccine against bordetella, another cause of kennel cough, can be given in droplet form down the nose prior to your dog entering boarding kennels. All these diseases are described on page 108.

- **Vaccinating puppies**

In the puppy, vaccination should start at eight to ten weeks of age, and is a course of two injections, two to four weeks apart. It is recommended that adult dogs have an annual health check and booster inoculation by the vet.

The day's food should be given at a regular time each day. Usually the adult dog will have one meal a day, at either breakfast time or teatime. Both are equally acceptable but ideally hard exercise should not be given within an hour of a full meal. Rather give a long walk and then feed on your return. Some dogs seem to like two smaller meals a day, and this is perfectly acceptable, provided that the total amount of food given is not excessive.

■ **Water**

Your Retriever should have a full bowl of clean, fresh water changed once or twice a day, and this should be permanently available. This is particularly important if he is on a complete dried food.

■ **Toileting**

Your dog should be let out into the garden first thing in the morning to toilet, and this can be taught quite easily on command and in a specified area of the garden. You should not take the dog out for a walk to toilet, unless you just do not have the space at home. The mess should be in your premises and then picked up and flushed down the toilet daily. Other people, children in particular, should not have to put up with our dogs' mess.

Throughout the day he should have access to a toileting area every few hours, and always last thing at night before you all turn in.

Dogs will usually want to, and can be conditioned to, defaecate immediately after a meal, so this should be encouraged.

■ **Company**

Retrievers are very sociable dogs and bond to you strongly. There is no point having one unless you intend to be there most of the time. Obviously a well trained and socialized adult should be capable of being left for one to three hours at a time, but puppies need constant attention if they are to grow up well

balanced. Games, as mentioned before, are an essential daily pastime.

■ **Dental care**

Some complete diets are very crunchy. These by mimicking the diet of a wild dog, e.g. a fox or a wolf, which will eat a whole rabbit (bones, fur etc.) will help keep your dog's teeth relatively free of plaque and tartar. However, a daily teeth inspection is sensible. Lift the lips and look at, not just the front incisor and canine teeth, but also the back premolars and molars. They should be a healthy, shiny white like ours.

If not, or if on a soft, canned or fresh meat diet, daily brushing using a toothbrush

## UNDERSHOT/OVERSHOT JAWS

Undershot/overshot jaws result in a misaligned bite which is usually normal in a short-nosed dog, but is a defect in others. No action is necessary unless the condition causes the dog discomfort when eating.

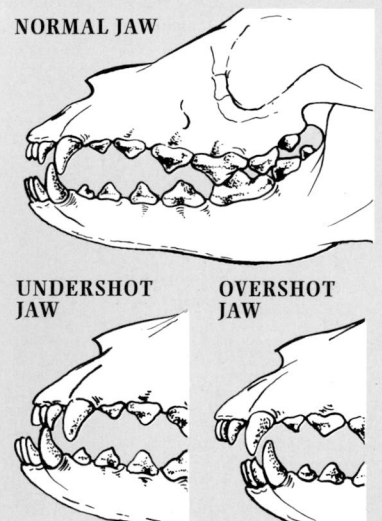

**NORMAL JAW**

**UNDERSHOT JAW**  **OVERSHOT JAW**

## TEETH AND JAWS

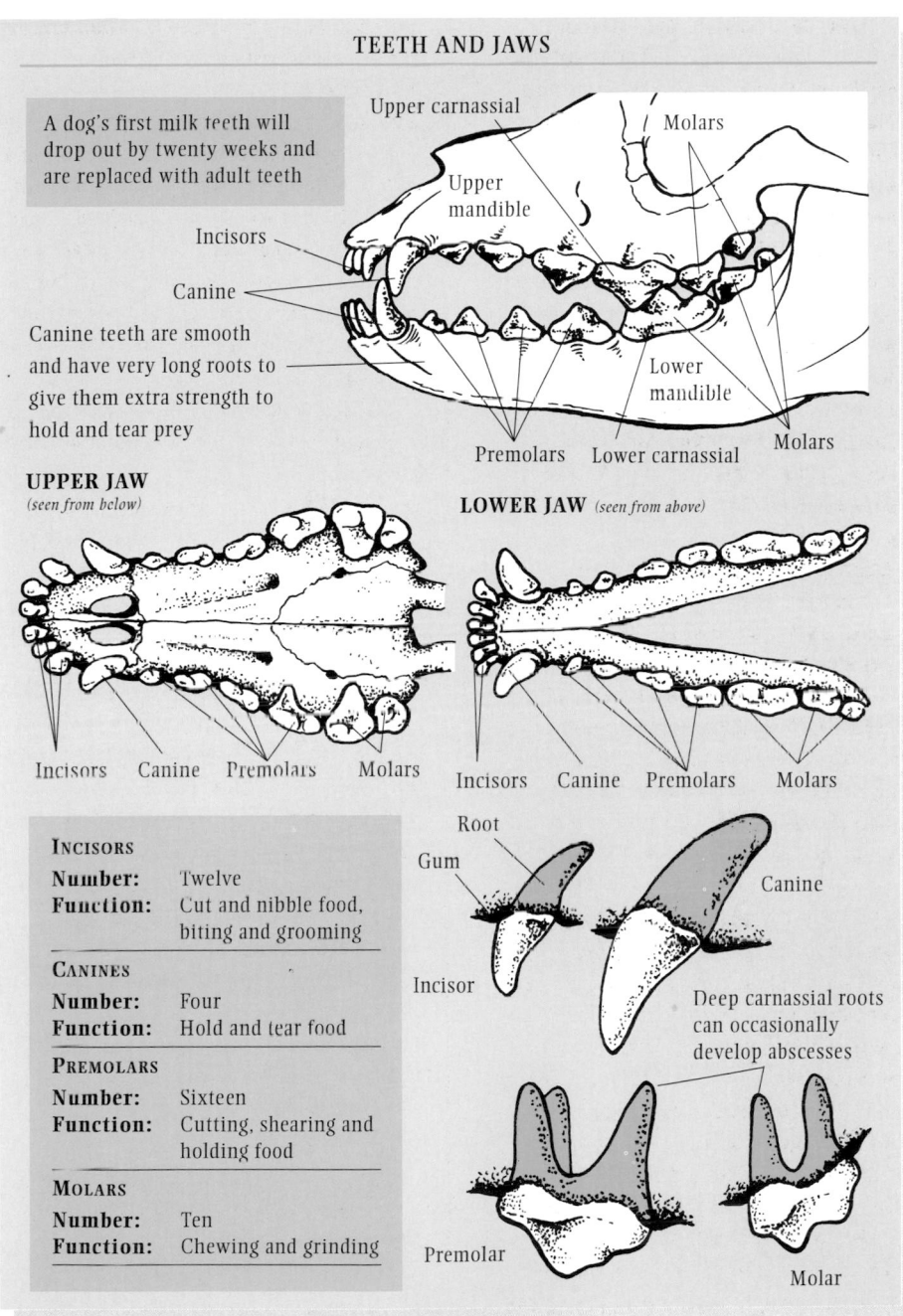

A dog's first milk teeth will drop out by twenty weeks and are replaced with adult teeth

Upper carnassial

Molars

Upper mandible

Incisors

Canine

Canine teeth are smooth and have very long roots to give them extra strength to hold and tear prey

Lower mandible

Premolars    Lower carnassial    Molars

**UPPER JAW**
*(seen from below)*

**LOWER JAW** *(seen from above)*

Incisors    Canine    Premolars    Molars

Incisors    Canine    Premolars    Molars

**INCISORS**
**Number:** Twelve
**Function:** Cut and nibble food, biting and grooming

**CANINES**
**Number:** Four
**Function:** Hold and tear food

**PREMOLARS**
**Number:** Sixteen
**Function:** Cutting, shearing and holding food

**MOLARS**
**Number:** Ten
**Function:** Chewing and grinding

Root

Gum

Canine

Incisor

Deep carnassial roots can occasionally develop abscesses

Premolar

Molar

and enzyme toothpaste is advisable. Hide chew sticks help clean teeth, as do root vegetables such as carrots, and many vets recommend a large raw marrow bone. These can, however, occasionally cause teeth to break. Various manufacturers have brought out tasty, chewy food items that benefit teeth, and your vet will be able to recommend a suitable one.

Pups are born with, or acquire shortly after birth, a full set of temporary teeth. These start to be shed at about sixteen weeks of age with the central incisors, and the transition from temporary to permanent teeth should be complete by six months of age. If extra teeth seem to be present, or if teeth seem out of position at this age, it is wise to see your vet.

## PERIODIC HEALTHCARE

## Worming

### ■ Roundworms (Toxocara)
All Retriever puppies should be wormed fortnightly from two weeks to three months of age, then monthly up to six months of age.

### WORMING YOUR DOG

Dogs need to be wormed regularly for roundworms:
- ■ Fortnightly for puppies from two weeks to three months of age
- ■ Monthly for puppies from three months to six months of age
- ■ Twice yearly thereafter in male dogs and neutered females

**Note:** bitches used for breeding have special requirements – ask your vet. Adult dogs should be wormed twice a year for tapeworms.

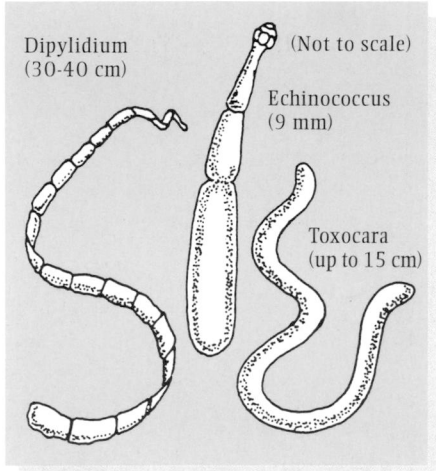

Dipylidium (30-40 cm)

(Not to scale)

Echinococcus (9 mm)

Toxocara (up to 15 cm)

Thereafter in a male or neutered female Retriever, you should worm twice yearly. Dogs used for breeding have special roundworming requirements and you should consult your vet about these. There is evidence that females undergoing false (pseudo) pregnancies have roundworm larvae migrating in their tissues, so they should be wormed at this time.

### ■ Tapeworms (Dipylidium and Echinococcus)
These need intermediate hosts (fleas and usually sheep offal respectively) to complete their life cycle, so prevention of contact with these is advisable. As a precaution, most vets recommend tapeworming adult dogs twice a year.

There are very effective, safe combined roundworm and tapeworm wormers available now from your vet.

## SPECIAL HEALTH PROBLEMS

Retrievers are usually fit, friendly and interesting companions. There are, however, some health problems that are known to occur

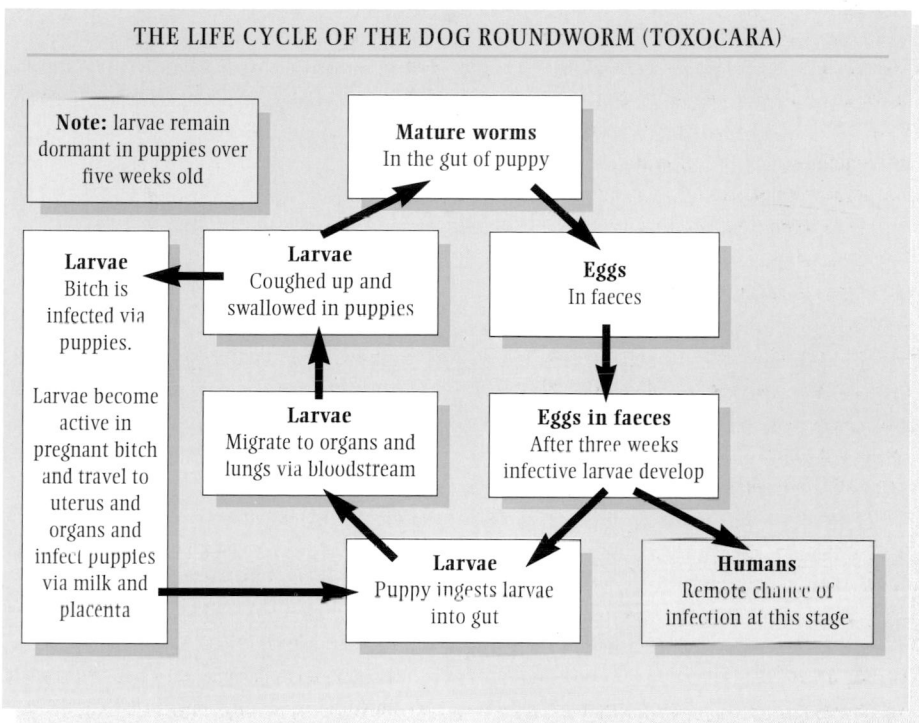

## THE LIFE CYCLE OF THE DOG ROUNDWORM (TOXOCARA)

**Note:** larvae remain dormant in puppies over five weeks old

**Mature worms**
In the gut of puppy

**Larvae**
Bitch is infected via puppies.

Larvae become active in pregnant bitch and travel to uterus and organs and infect puppies via milk and placenta

**Larvae**
Coughed up and swallowed in puppies

**Eggs**
In faeces

**Larvae**
Migrate to organs and lungs via bloodstream

**Eggs in faeces**
After three weeks infective larvae develop

**Larvae**
Puppy ingests larvae into gut

**Humans**
Remote chance of infection at this stage

in this breed particularly. A few of the commoner problems are detailed below.

■ **Hip dysplasia**

Hip dysplasia is the most common inherited disease of the Retrievers, especially Goldens (see page 127). It is a malformation of one or both hip joints, and may not be detectable until the dog is a young adult or even older. Stiffness on rising, an odd bunny-hopping gait or lameness are the usual signs. Reduce the chances of your dog being affected by checking the hip scores of the puppy's parents, and by keeping exercise to a gentle level until your dog is at least six months old.

■ **Cataract**

This is an opacity of the lens in one or both eyes. The pupil appears greyish instead of the normal black colour. In advanced cases the lens looks like a pearl and the dog may be blind. The many causes of cataract in Retrievers include inherited causes, infection, diabetes mellitus, and trauma.

■ **Central Progressive Retinal Atrophy (CPRA)**

This is an inherited progressive degeneration of the retina of the eye, found in the Golden Retriever and other breeds, which may lead to total blindness. Affected dogs of either sex must not be used for breeding.

This disease is covered more fully on page 119 under Eye Diseases.

■ **Entropion**

This is an inherited disease, usually of the young, growing dog, seen quite often in the

Golden Retriever. The edge of an eyelid rolls in so that the lashes rub against the surface of the eye, causing irritation of the eyeball. The eye is sore and wet with tears, and often kept closed. Surgical treatment is necessary.

■ **von Willebrand's disease**

An inherited disease of another blood component, the platelets, causing haemorrhage is known to occur in the Golden Retriever.

■ **Corneal lipidosis**

This is a small white deposit of fats in the cornea of the eye, and is seen quite often in the Golden Retriever. The appearence is that of a small white spot on the front surface of the eye, usually roughly circular, usually followed shortly by a similar blemish in the other eye. Vision is not usually affected, and no treatment is necessary.

■ **Primary glaucoma**

This is inherited in the Golden and Flat Coated Retrievers and some other breeds and is caused by an increase in the pressure of the aqueous humour fluid inside the eye. It is often sudden in onset. The affected eye becomes enlarged, inflamed and painful as the pressure increases. If untreated, the eye becomes grossly enlarged and eyesight fails.

Treatment is never easy. Topical drops can be used to constrict the pupil which aids the removal of aqueous humour, whilst at the same time drugs are given to try to reduce its production. In many cases surgery is required to establish drainage of the eye. In extreme cases the eye must be surgically removed.

■ **Epilepsy**

This is a condition that is seen more often in the Golden Retriever than some breeds. The dog has a sudden, unexpected fit or a convulsion, which lasts for about two minutes. Recovery is fairly quick, although the dog may be dull and look confused for a few hours.

Treatment is usually necessary and successful as far as control of epilepsy is concerned.

■ **Osteochondrosis dissicans (OCD)**

This is a degeneration of the cartilage in certain joints of young dogs under a year old, seen occasionally in the Retrievers. Surgical removal of the affected cartilage is usually necessary. OCD is dealt with more fully in Chapter 9.

**Important:** in addition to the specific advice given above, reduce the chances of your new dog having these problems by asking the right questions about his ancestry before you purchase him. Apart from hip dysplasia (in all three Retrievers), cataract, central progressive retinal atrophy, primary glaucoma (in Golden and Flat Coats) and entropion, all the above problems are uncommon.

## PET HEALTH INSURANCE AND VETS' FEES

By choosing wisely to start with, and then ensuring that your dog is fit, the right weight, occupied both mentally and physically, protected against disease by vaccination, and fed correctly, you should minimize any vet's bills. The unexpected may well happen though. Accidents and injuries occur, and Retrievers can develop lifelong allergies, or long-term illnesses or problems such as HD, OCD, or diabetes. Pet health insurance is available and is recommended by the vast majority of veterinarians for such unexpected eventualities. It is important to take out a policy that will suit you and your Retriever, so it is wise to ask your veterinary surgeon for his recommendation.

# DISEASES AND ILLNESSES

## RESPIRATORY DISEASES

### ■ Rhinitis

Rhinitis, an infection of the nose caused by viruses, bacteria or fungi, is fairly common in the Retriever. It may also be part of a disease such as distemper or kennel cough. Sneezing or a clear or coloured discharge are the usual signs. Another cause, due to the dog's habit of sniffing, is a grass seed or other foreign object inhaled through the nostrils. The dog starts to sneeze violently, often after a walk through long grass.

### ■ Tumours of the nose

Tumours of the nose are also fairly common in the Retriever. The first sign is often haemorrhage from one nostril. X-rays reveal a mass in the nasal chamber.

### ■ Laryngeal paralysis

This is a disease of the old dog, and is seen more in the various Retrievers than in other breeds. The vocal cords become paralysed, obstruct the airway and vibrate on inspiration, causing loud, noisy breathing on both inhaling and exhaling. Surgery is needed to correct this.

## THE RESPIRATORY SYSTEM

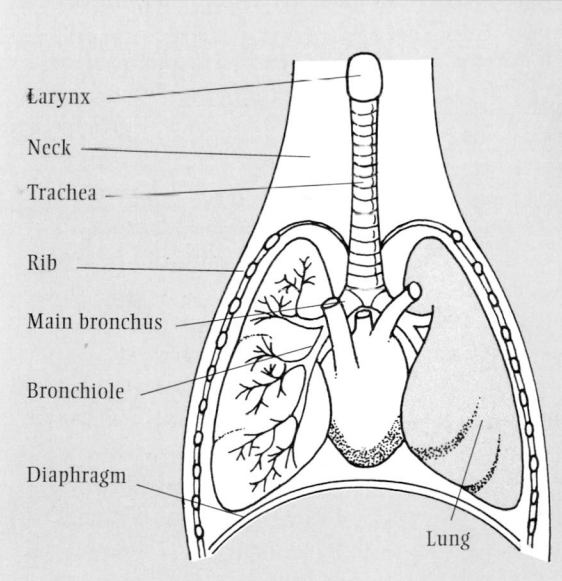

Larynx

Neck

Trachea

Rib

Main bronchus

Bronchiole

Diaphragm

Lung

The larynx, trachea, lungs and bronchi, together with the nose, make up the dog's respiratory system. Air is inhaled through the nose, filtered and passed through the larynx into the trachea. It enters the lungs through the bronchi, which subdivide into bronchioles and end in alveoli, or air sacs. Oxygen and carbon dioxide gases are exchanged in the alveoli.

## INFECTIOUS DISEASES

■ **Distemper (hardpad)**

This is a frequently fatal virus disease which usually affects dogs under one year of age. Affected dogs cough and have a discharge from the eyes and nose. Pneumonia often develops, and vomiting and diarrhoea usually follows. If the dog lives, nervous symptoms, such as fits, paralysis, or chorea (a type of regular twitch), are likely. The pads of the feet become thickened and hard – hence the other name for the disease, hardpad.

■ **Treatment** by antibiotics sometimes helps, but the only real answer is prevention by vaccination as a puppy, and annual boosters.

■ **Infectious canine hepatitis**

This affects the liver. In severe cases, the first sign may be a dog completely off his food, very depressed and collapsed. Some die suddenly. Recovery is unlikely from this severe form of the disease. Prevention by vaccination is essential.

■ **Leptospirosis**

Two separate diseases affect dogs. Both, in addition to causing severe and often fatal disease in the dog, are infectious to humans. **Leptospira canicola** causes acute kidney disease in dogs.

**Leptospira icterohaemorrhagiae** causes an acute infection of the liver, often leading to jaundice.

■ **Treatment** of both is often unsuccessful, and prevention by vaccination is essential.

■ **Canine parvovirus**

This affects the bowels causing a sudden onset of vomiting and diarrhoea, often with blood, and severe depression. As death is usually due to dehydration, prompt replacement of the fluid and electrolyte loss is essential. In addition, antibiotics are also usually given to prevent secondary bacterial infection. Prevention by vaccination is essential.

■ **Kennel cough**

This highly infectious cough occurs mainly in kennelled dogs. It can be caused by:

■ Bordetella, a bacterial infection

■ Parainfluenza virus

Both of these affect the trachea and lungs. Occasionally, a purulent discharge from the nose and eyes may develop. Antibiotics and rest are usually prescribed by the vet. Prevention of both diseases by vaccination is highly recommended.

## Diseases producing a cough

A cough is a reflex which clears foreign matter from the bronchi, trachea and larynx. Severe inflammation of these structures will also stimulate the cough reflex.

■ **Laryngitis, tracheitis and bronchitis**

Inflammation of these structures can be caused by infection such as kennel cough or canine distemper, by irritant fumes or by foreign material. Usually, all three parts of the airway are affected at the same time.

Bronchitis is a major problem in the older dog caused by a persistent infection or irritation, producing irreversible changes in the bronchi. A cough develops and increases until the dog seems to cough almost constantly.

## Diseases producing laboured breathing

Laboured breathing is normally caused by those diseases which occupy space within the chest, and reduce the lung tissue available for oxygenation of the blood. An X-ray produces an accurate diagnosis.

- **Pneumonia**

This is an infection of the lungs caused by viruses, bacteria, fungi or foreign material. It can occur in Retrievers but it is uncommon.

- **Chest tumours**

These can cause respiratory problems by occupying lung space and by causing the accumulation of fluid within the chest.

## Accidents

Respiratory failure commonly follows accidents. Several types of injury may be seen.

- **Haemorrhage into the lung**

Rupture of a blood vessel in the lung will release blood which fills the air sacs.

- **Ruptured diaphragm**

This allows abdominal organs such as the liver, spleen or stomach to move forward into the chest cavity.

### HEART AND CIRCULATION DISEASES

**Heart attack** in the human sense is uncommon. Collapse or fainting may occur due to inadequate cardiac function.

## Heart murmurs

- **Acquired disease**

This may result from wear and tear or inflammation of heart valves, problems of

rhythm and rate, or disease of the heart muscle. Signs of disease may include the following symptoms: weakness, lethargy, panting, cough, abdominal distension, collapse, and weight loss.

- **Congenital heart disease**

Congenital heart diseases his is usually due to valve defects or a hole in the heart. Signs of disease may include the sudden death of a

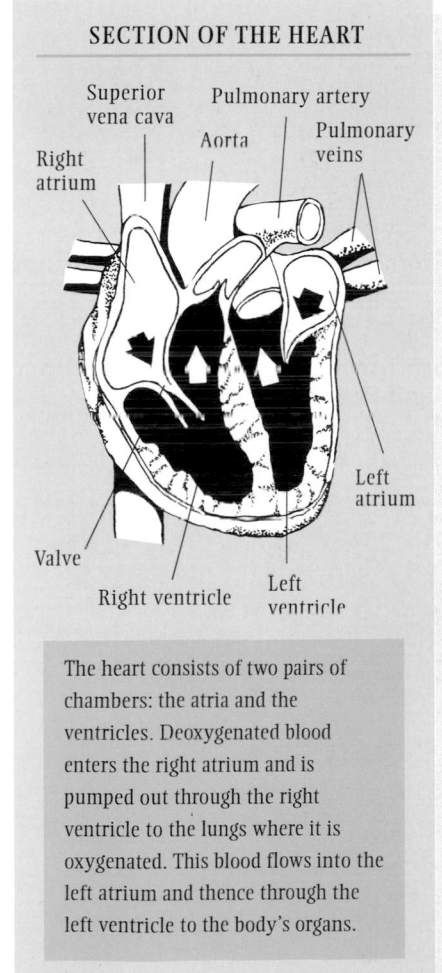

### SECTION OF THE HEART

Superior vena cava, Pulmonary artery, Aorta, Pulmonary veins, Right atrium, Left atrium, Valve, Right ventricle, Left ventricle

The heart consists of two pairs of chambers: the atria and the ventricles. Deoxygenated blood enters the right atrium and is pumped out through the right ventricle to the lungs where it is oxygenated. This blood flows into the left atrium and thence through the left ventricle to the body's organs.

## THE CIRCULATORY SYSTEM

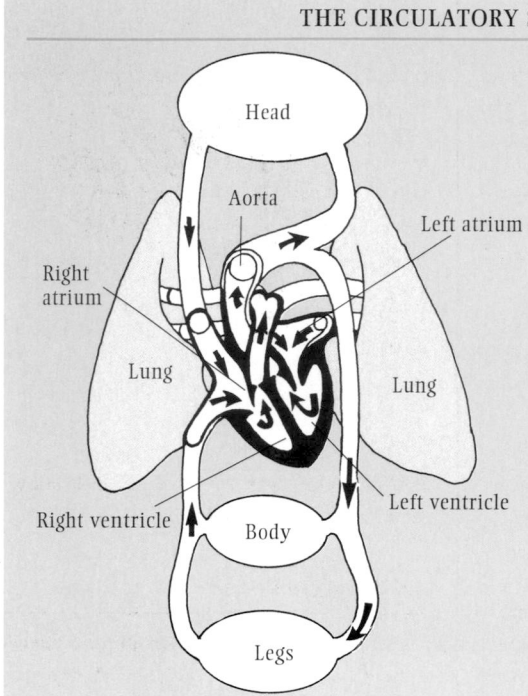

Head

Aorta

Left atrium

Right atrium

Lung

Lung

Right ventricle

Left ventricle

Body

Legs

Blood circulates around the dog's body by way of the circulatory system.

■ Oxygenated blood is pumped by the heart through the arteries to all the body organs, e.g. the brain, muscles and liver.

■ Oxygen and nutrients are extracted from the blood.

■ The used blood is returned by the veins to the right ventricle and then to the lungs.

■ In the lungs, carbon dioxide is exchanged for oxygen.

---

pup, or weakness and failure to thrive or grow at a normal rate.

■ **Congestive heart failure** is the end result of any of these defects.

## Heart block

This is an acquired problem. A nerve impulse conduction failure occurs in the specialized heart muscle responsible for maintaining normal rhythm and rate.

## Blood clotting defects

■ **Clotting problems** may result from poisoning with Warfarin rat poison. Haemorrhage occurs (see page 133).

### SIGNS OF HEART FAILURE

These may include the following:
■ Exercise intolerance
■ Lethargy
■ Panting and/or cough
■ Enlargement of the abdomen due to fluid accumulation
■ Poor digestion and weight loss
  Veterinary investigation involves thorough examination, possibly X-rays of the chest, ECG and, in some cases, ultrasound scanning.

■ **Congenital clotting defects** arise if the pup is born with abnormal blood platelets or clotting factors, both of which are essential in normal clotting.

- **von Willebrand's disease** is an inherited platelet disorder sometimes found in Retrievers.

## Tumours

The spleen, which is a reservoir for blood, is a relatively common site for tumours, especially in older dogs. Splenic tumours can bleed slowly into the abdomen or rupture suddenly in the active Retriever, causing collapse. Surgical removal of the spleen is necessary.

### DIGESTIVE SYSTEM DISEASES

## Mouth problems

### Dental disease

- **Dental tartar** forms on the tooth surfaces when left over food (plaque) solidifies on the teeth. This irritates the adjacent gum, causing pain, mouth odour, gum recession, and ultimately tooth loss. This inevitable progression to periodontal disease may be prevented if plaque is removed by regular tooth brushing coupled with good diet, large chews and hard biscuits.

- **Periodontal disease** is inflammation and erosion of the gums around the tooth roots. It is less of a problem in large breeds like the Retriever, but does occur. Careful scaling and polishing of the teeth by your vet under an anaesthetic is necessary to save the teeth.

- **Dental caries** (tooth decay) is common in people, but not so in dogs unless they are given chocolate.

- **Tooth fractures** can result from trauma in road accidents or if your dog is an enthusiastic stone catcher or chewer. A root treatment may be needed.

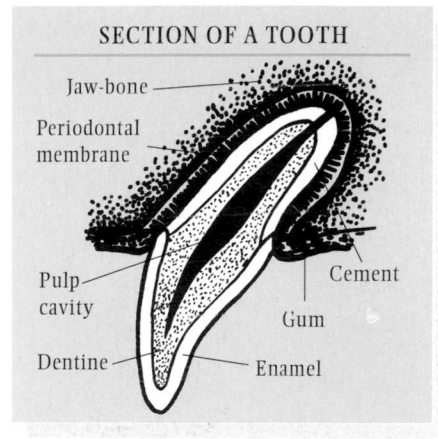

**SECTION OF A TOOTH**

Jaw-bone

Periodontal membrane

Pulp cavity

Cement

Gum

Dentine

Enamel

- **Epulis** is a benign overgrowth of the gum. Surgical removal is needed.

## Salivary cysts

These may occur as swellings under the tongue or neck, resulting from a ruptured salivary duct. Surgical removal is usually necessary.

## Mouth tumours

These are often highly malignant, growing rapidly and spreading to other organs. First symptoms may be bad breath, increased salivation, and bleeding from the mouth plus difficulties in eating.

## Foreign bodies in the mouth

(See First Aid, page 138)

## Problems causing vomiting

- **Gastritis**

This is inflammation of the stomach and can result from an unsuitable diet, scavenging or

## THE DIGESTIVE SYSTEM

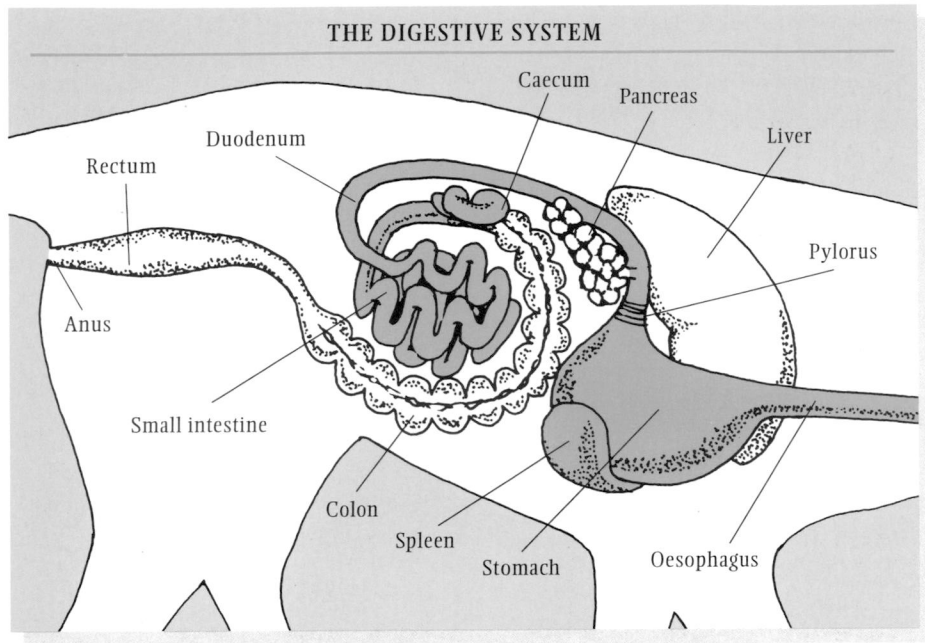

infection. The dog repeatedly vomits either food or yellowish fluid and froth, which may be blood stained.

■ **Obstruction of the oesophagus**

This leads to the regurgitation of food immediately after feeding, and may be caused by small bones or other foreign bodies. Diagnosis is confirmed either by X-ray or examination with an endoscope, and treatment must not be delayed.

■ **Obstruction lower down the gut, in the stomach or intestine**

This may result from items such as stones, corks etc. Tumours can also lead to obstructive vomiting. The dog rapidly becomes very ill and the diagnosis is usually confirmed by palpation, X-rays or exploratory surgery.

■ **Intussusception**

This is telescoping of the bowel which can follow diarrhoea. Surgery is essential.

■ **Gastric dilation**

(See First Aid, page 139)

■ **Megoesophagus**

This a defect in the wall of the oesophagus due to faulty nerve control, which leads to ballooning, retention of swallowed food and regurgitation before the food reaches the stomach. It is readily diagnosed by X-ray.

## Pancreatic diseases

■ **Acute pancreatitis**

This is an extremely painful and serious condition requiring intensive therapy. It can be life-threatening.

■ **Pancreatic insufficiency**

Wasting of the cells of the pancreas which produce digestive enzymes leads to poor digestive function, persistent diarrhoea, weight loss and ravenous appetite. The condition,

## PROBLEMS CAUSING DIARRHOEA

- **Dietary diarrhoea**

This can occur as a result of sudden changes in diet, scavenging, feeding unsuitable foods or stress (especially in pups when they go to their new home).

- **Pancreatic insufficiency** (opposite)
- **Malabsorption**

This is an uncommon condition leading to defective absorption of digested food. Affected dogs have ravenous appetite, pass bulky, soft faeces, and are underweight. Laboratory tests are often required to confirm the diagnosis.

- **Enteritis**

This is inflammation of the small intestines which can be caused by infection, e.g. parvovirus, a severe worm burden or food poisoning. Continued diarrhoea leads to dehydration.

- **Colitis**

An inflammation of the large bowel (colon). The symptoms include straining and frequent defaecation, watery faeces with mucous or blood, and often an otherwise healthy dog.

- **Tumours of the bowel**

These are more likely to cause vomiting than diarrhoea, but one which is called lymphosarcoma causes diffuse thickening of the gut lining which may lead to diarrhoea.

- **Diabetes mellitus**

Another function of the pancreas is to manufacture the hormone insulin, which controls blood sugar levels. If insulin is deficient, blood and urine glucose levels rise, both of which can be detected on laboratory testing. Affected animals have an increased appetite and thirst, weight loss and lethargy. If left untreated the dog may go into a diabetic coma.

- **Pancreatic tumours**

These are relatively common and are usually highly malignant. Symptoms vary from vomiting, weight loss and signs of abdominal pain to acute jaundice. The prognosis is usually hopeless, and death rapidly occurs.

## LIVER DISEASES

- **Acute hepatitis** – infectious canine hepatitis and leptospirosis (see Infectious Diseases, page 108). It is not common as most dogs are vaccinated.
- **Chronic liver failure**

This can be due to heart failure, tumours or cirrhosis. Affected dogs usually lose weight and become depressed, off their food and may vomit. Diarrhoea and increased thirst are other possible symptoms. The liver may increase or decrease in size, and there is sometimes fluid retention in the abdomen. Jaundice is sometimes apparent. Diagnosis of liver disease depends on symptoms, blood tests, X-rays or ultrasound examination, and possibly liver biopsy.

## SKIN DISEASES

### Itchy skin diseases

**Parasites**

- **Fleas** are the commonest cause of skin disease, and dogs often become allergic to

when it occurs, is often diagnosed in dogs of less than two years of age, and is occasionally seen in the Retriever. Diagnosis is made on clinical symptoms and laboratory testing of blood and faeces.

them. They are dark, fast moving, sideways flattened insects, about two millimetres long. They spend about two hours a day feeding on the dog, then jump off and spend the rest of the day breeding and laying eggs. They live for about three weeks and can lay up to fifty eggs a day. Thus each flea may leave behind up to 1000 eggs which hatch out in as little as three weeks. It is important to treat the dog with an effective, modern veterinary product, and also the environment, i.e. your house.

Fleas seem to be developing a resistance to the traditional insecticide treatments, but there is a range of 'second generation' products available on prescription from your vet which are extremely effective yet may be applied only

## TUMOURS AND CYSTS

■ **Sebaceous cysts**
These are round, painless nodules in the skin and vary from 2 mm up to 4 cm in diameter. They are seen in the Retriever, particularly as they get older.

■ **Warts**
Warts are quite common in the older dog, and, along with other skin tumours, do occur in Retrievers.

■ **Anal adenomas**
These frequently develop around the anus in old un-neutered male dogs. They ulcerate when they are quite small and produce small bleeding points.

## PARASITES

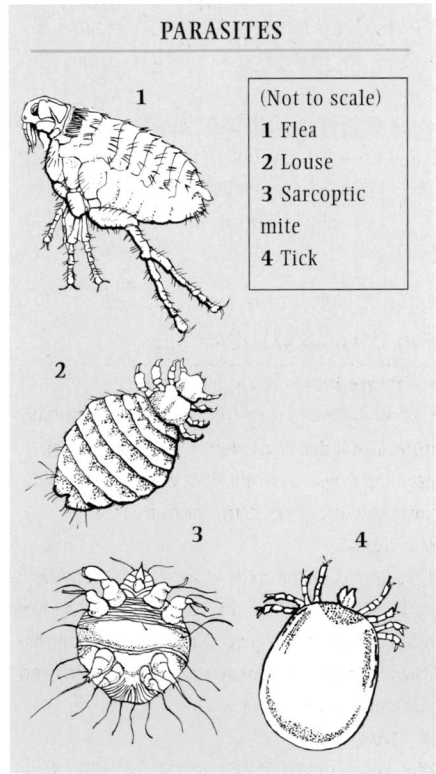

(Not to scale)
**1** Flea
**2** Louse
**3** Sarcoptic mite
**4** Tick

every two to three months to the dog, and once or twice a year to the carpets and chairs etc. They also kill lice, ticks, and most mites.

■ **Lice** are small, whitish insects which crawl very slowly between and up the hairs. They lay eggs on the hair, spend their entire life on the dog and are less common and much easier to treat than fleas.

■ **Mange** is caused by mites (usually Sarcoptes) which burrow into the skin, causing intense irritation and hair loss. It is very contagious and more common in young dogs. Treatment is by anti-parasitic washes.

■ **Bacterial infections**
These are common in the dog and are often secondary to some other skin disease, such as mange or allergies.

**Pyoderma** can be an acute, wet, painful area of the skin (wet eczema), or a more persistent infection appearing as ring-like sores. Both are very common in the Retriever.

**Furunculosis** is a deeper, more serious

## STRUCTURE OF THE SKIN

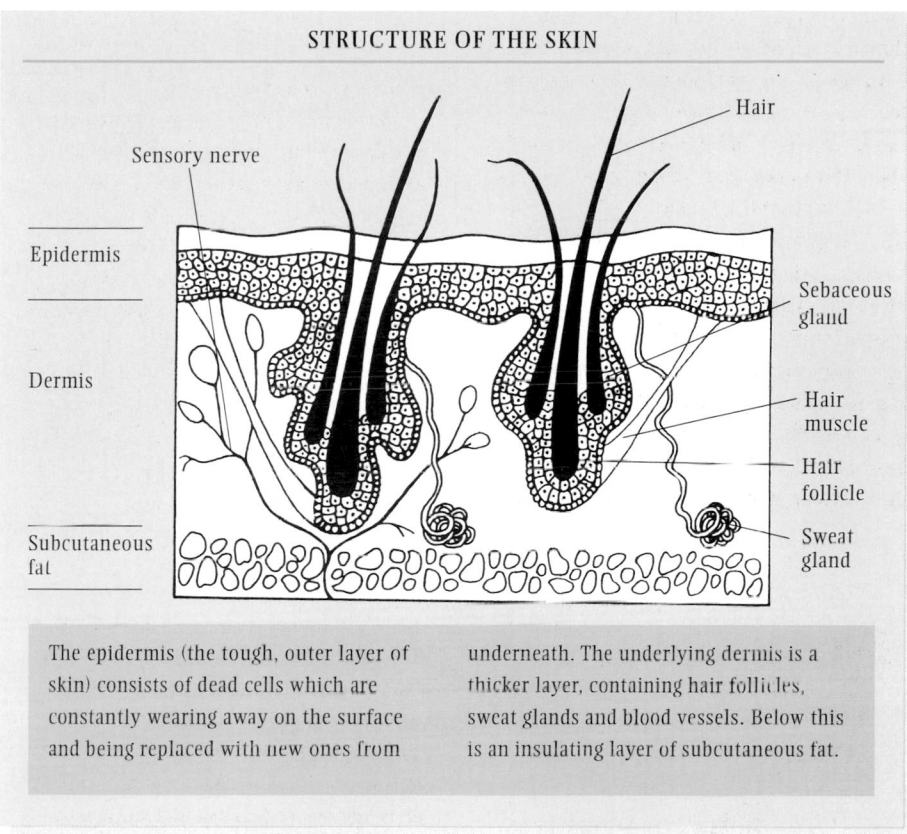

The epidermis (the tough, outer layer of skin) consists of dead cells which are constantly wearing away on the surface and being replaced with new ones from underneath. The underlying dermis is a thicker layer, containing hair follicles, sweat glands and blood vessels. Below this is an insulating layer of subcutaneous fat.

infection seen less often in the Retriever.

**Contact dermatitis** is an itchy reddening of the skin, usually of the abdomen, groin, armpit, or feet, where the hair is thinnest and less protective. It can be an allergic response to materials, such as wool, nylon or carpets, or to a direct irritant, such as oil, or a disinfectant.

■ **Lick granuloma**

This is a thickened, hairless patch of skin, usually seen on the front of the wrist or the side of the ankle. It is quite common in the Retriever and is thought to result from constant licking of this area because of boredom or neurosis.

## Non-itchy skin diseases

■ **Demodectic mange**

Caused by a congenitally-transmitted parasitic mite, Demodectic mange is seen usually in growing dogs, and causes non-itchy patchy hair loss. It is very difficult to treat.

■ **Ticks**

These are parasitic spiders that attach themselves to the skin. They drop off after a week when they resemble small grey peas, but should be removed when noticed. Soak them with surgical spirit and pull out using fine tweezers.

■ **Ringworm**

This is a fungal infection of the hairs and skin

causing bald patches. It is transmissible to people, especially children.

■ **Hormonal skin disease**

This patchy, symmetrical hair loss is quite common in the Retriever.

## DISEASES OF THE ANAL AREA

■ **Anal sac impaction**

This is quite common in the Retriever. The anal sacs are scent glands and little used in the dog. If the secretion slowly accumulates in the gland instead of being emptied during defaecation, the overful anal sac become itchy. The dog drags his anus along the ground or bites himself around the base of his tail. Unless the sacs are emptied by your vet, an abscess may form.

## DISEASES OF THE FEET

■ **Interdigital eczema**

Retrievers readily lick their feet after minor damage, and this makes the feet very wet. Infection then occurs between the pads.

■ **Interdigital cysts and abscesses**

These are painful swellings between the toes which may make the dog lame. In most cases the cause is unknown, but sometimes they can

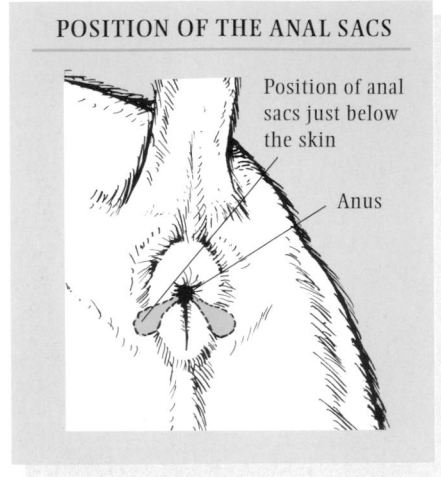

**POSITION OF THE ANAL SACS**

Position of anal sacs just below the skin

Anus

be caused by a grass seed penetrating the skin between the toes.

■ **Foreign body in the pad**

The most common foreign body is a sharp fragment of glass, or thorn. The dog is usually very lame and the affected pad painful to the touch. Often an entry point will be seen on the pad.

■ **Nail bed infections**

The toe becomes swollen and painful and the dog lame. The bone may become diseased and this can lead to amputation of the affected toe.

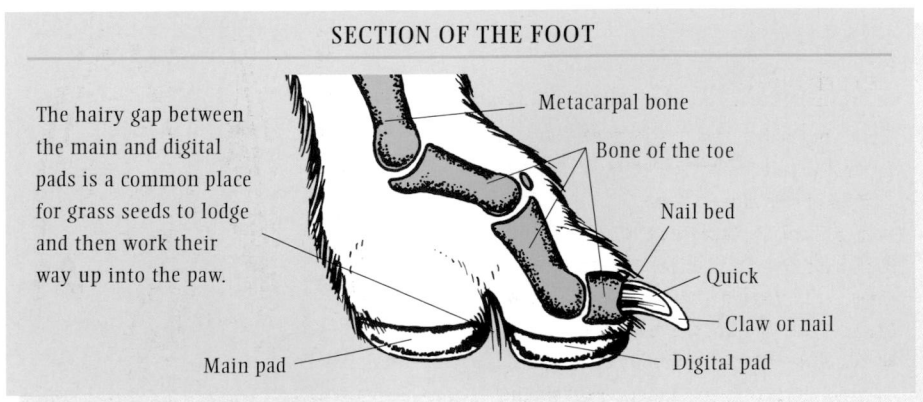

**SECTION OF THE FOOT**

The hairy gap between the main and digital pads is a common place for grass seeds to lodge and then work their way up into the paw.

Metacarpal bone

Bone of the toe

Nail bed

Quick

Claw or nail

Digital pad

Main pad

## STRUCTURE OF THE FEET

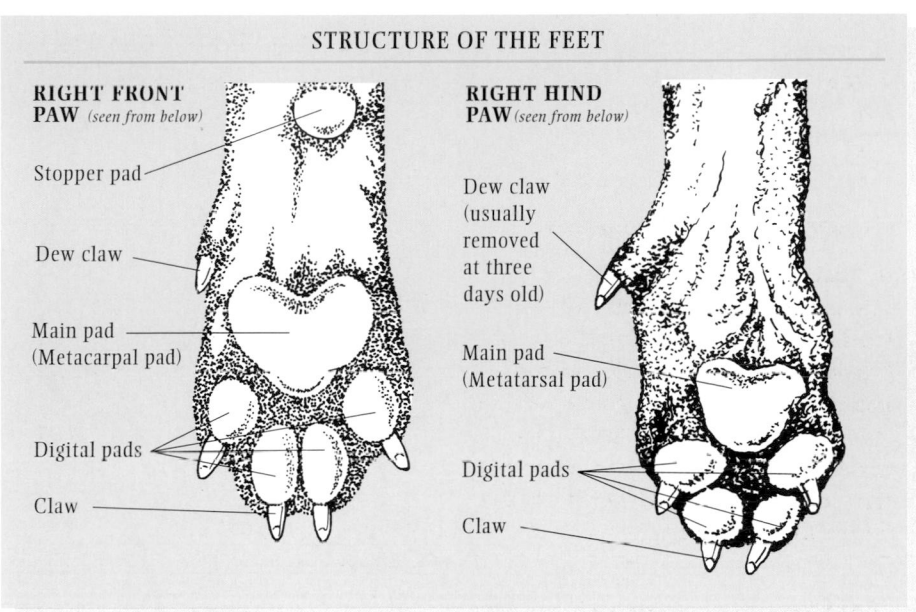

**RIGHT FRONT PAW** *(seen from below)*

Stopper pad

Dew claw

Main pad
(Metacarpal pad)

Digital pads

Claw

**RIGHT HIND PAW** *(seen from below)*

Dew claw
(usually
removed
at three
days old)

Main pad
(Metatarsal pad)

Digital pads

Claw

## EAR DISEASES

### Haematoma

This is a painless, sometimes large blood blister in the ear flap, usually caused by head shaking due to an ear infection or irritation. They seem to occur quite commonly in the Retriever, and surgery is usually necessary.

### Infection (otitis)

Due to his folded-over and hairy ear flap, and reduced ventilation of the ear, the Retriever is fairly prone to ear infections. When otitis occurs, a smelly discharge appears, and the dog shakes his head or scratches his ear. If the inner ear is affected, the dog may also show a head tilt or a disturbance in his balance.

■ **Treatment** with antibiotic ear drops is usually successful, but sometimes syringing or a surgical operation is needed. The vet must be consulted as there are several possible reasons for ear disease including ear mites and grass seeds.

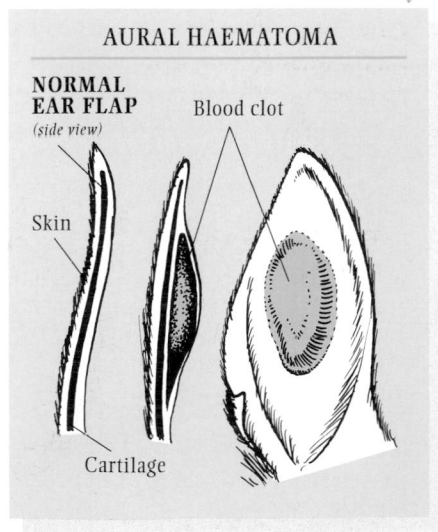

### AURAL HAEMATOMA

**NORMAL EAR FLAP**
*(side view)*

Blood clot

Skin

Cartilage

## STRUCTURE OF THE EAR

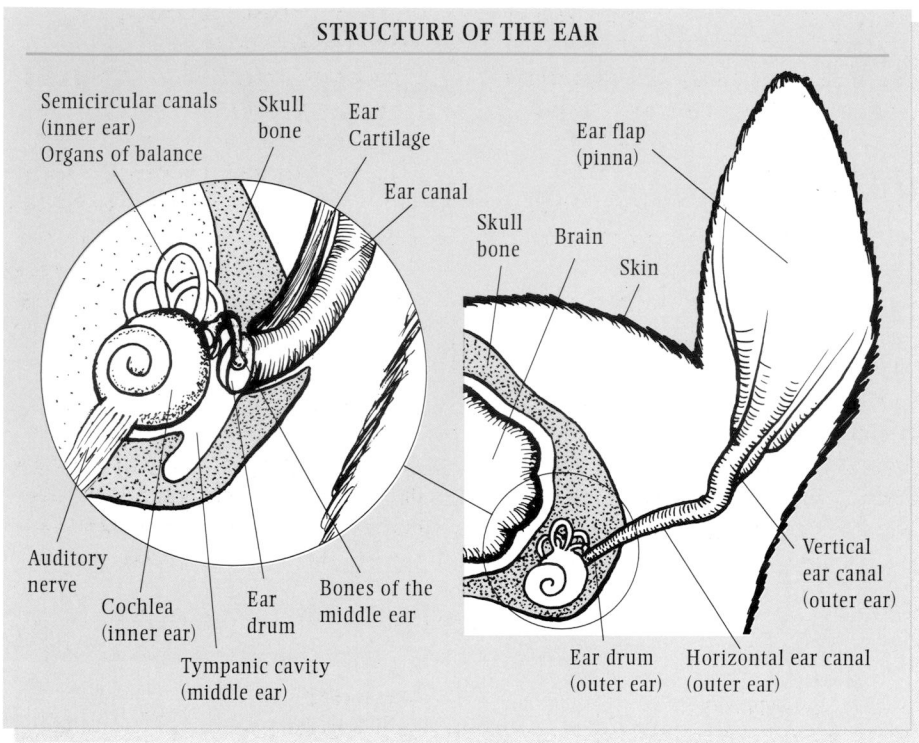

Semicircular canals (inner ear) Organs of balance

Skull bone

Ear Cartilage

Ear canal

Ear flap (pinna)

Skull bone

Brain

Skin

Auditory nerve

Cochlea (inner ear)

Ear drum

Bones of the middle ear

Tympanic cavity (middle ear)

Ear drum (outer ear)

Horizontal ear canal (outer ear)

Vertical ear canal (outer ear)

## EYE DISEASES

### Entropion

This is an inherited disease, usually of the young, growing dog, seen quite often in the Retriever. The edge of an eyelid rolls in so that the lashes rub against the surface of the eye, causing irritation of the eyeball. The eye is sore and wet with tears, and often kept closed. Surgical treatment is necessary.

### Keratitis

This is a very sore inflammation of the cornea which may appear blue and lose its shiny appearance.

### Third eyelid disease

Two problems occasionally occur in Retrievers. These are as follows:
- **Prolapse of the Harderian gland**
This is a small fleshy mass of tissue behind the third eyelid. It can become displaced and protrude. Surgical removal is necessary.
- **Eversion of the third eyelid**
Occasionally in young dogs, the edge of the nictitating membrane rolls outwards. It is unsightly and irritates the eye. The rolled-over tissue should be removed.

### Prolapse of the eye

(See First Aid, page 138)

## Progressive retinal atrophy (PRA)

This is an inherited progressive degeneration of the retina of the eye which may lead to total blindness. There are two types of PRA:

- **Generalised**
- **Central,** which is the type usually found in the Retriever. Both usually develop in the young adult.

There is no treatment for PRA and the disease must be controlled by the testing of breeding dogs.

**Note:** for many years now, the British Veterinary Association (BVA) in conjunction with the Kennel Club, have run the BVA/KC Eye Scheme to test all potential show and breeding Retrievers (and other breeds). Members of their Eye Panel, which consists of veterinary surgeons who have expertise and post-graduate qualifications in Ophthalmology, examine dogs referred from practising vets, and at dog shows, and issue Eye Certificates to show whether the dog is free from PRA, hereditary cataract, and other inherited eye diseases. All Retrievers intended for breeding should be examined by a vet on the BVA/Kennel Club Eye Panel before mating. Affected dogs of either sex must not be used for breeding.

## Conjunctivitis

This is common in the Retriever. The white of the eye appears red and discharges. Possible causes include viruses, bacteria, chemicals, allergies, trauma or foreign bodies.

### THE EYE

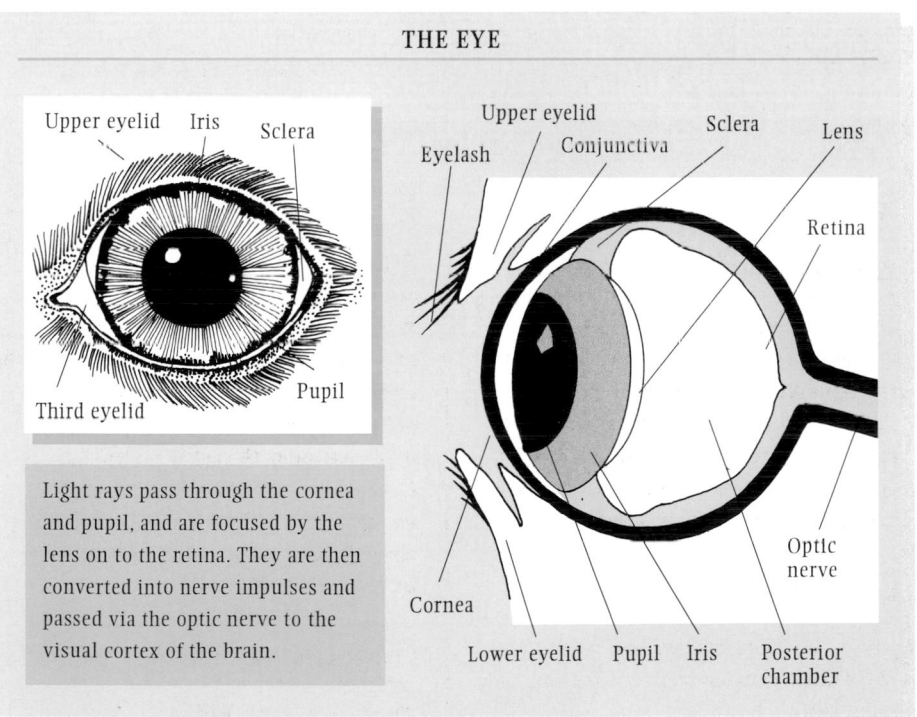

Upper eyelid  Iris  Sclera
Third eyelid  Pupil

Light rays pass through the cornea and pupil, and are focused by the lens on to the retina. They are then converted into nerve impulses and passed via the optic nerve to the visual cortex of the brain.

Upper eyelid  Conjunctiva  Sclera  Lens
Eyelash
Retina
Optic nerve
Cornea
Lower eyelid  Pupil  Iris  Posterior chamber

## Corneal ulcer

This is erosion of part of the surface of the cornea and can follow an injury or keratitis.

## Pannus

This is an autoimmune inflammation of the cornea. It occurs in some older Retrievers.

## Cataract

An opacity of the lens in one or both eyes. The pupil appears greyish instead of the normal black colour. In advanced cases the lens looks like a pearl and the dog may be blind. The many causes of cataract in Retrievers include inherited causes, infection, diabetes mellitus, and trauma. Surgical correction is possible to restore sight, unless PRA is also present.

## URINARY SYSTEM DISEASES

## Diseases producing increased thirst

■ **Acute kidney failure**
The most common infectious agent producing acute nephritis is Leptospirosis (see Infectious Diseases, page 108).
■ **Chronic kidney failure**
This is common in old dogs and occurs when persistent damage to the kidney results in toxic substances starting to accumulate in the blood stream.

## Diseases causing blood in the urine

■ **Cystitis**
This is an infection of the bladder. It is more common in the bitch because the infection has easy access through the shorter urethra. The clinical signs include increased frequency

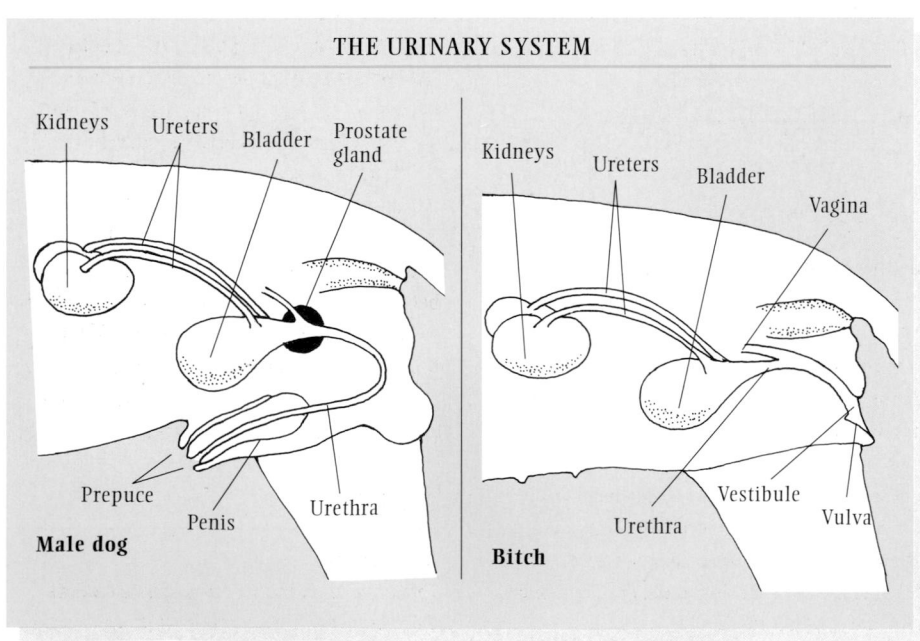

## THE URINARY SYSTEM

Kidneys   Ureters   Bladder   Prostate gland

Prepuce   Penis   Urethra

**Male dog**

Kidneys   Ureters   Bladder   Vagina

Vestibule   Vulva   Urethra

**Bitch**

of urination, straining and sometimes a bloody urine. In all other respects the dog remains healthy.

- **Urinary calculi or stones**
These can form in either the kidney or bladder.
- **Kidney stones** are small stones which can enter the ureters causing severe abdominal pain.
- **Bladder stones**, or calculi, are fairly common in both sexes. In the bitch they are larger and straining is usually the only clinical sign. In the dog the most common sign is unproductive straining due to urinary obstruction.
- **Tumours of the bladder**
These occur and cause frequent straining and bloody urine, or, by occupying space within the bladder, cause incontinence.

## Incontinence

Occasionally, this occurs for no apparent reason, and the older female Retriever can be affected. Hormones or medicine to tighten the bladder sphincter can help.

## REPRODUCTIVE ORGAN DISEASES

## The male dog

- **Retained testicle** (cryptorchidism)
Occasionally one or both testicles may fail to descend into the scrotum and remain somewhere along their developmental path. Surgery is advisable to remove retained testicles as they are very likely to develop cancer.
- **Tumours**
These are fairly common but, fortunately, most are benign. One type of testicular tumour, known as a Sertoli cell tumour, produces female hormones leading to the development of female characteristics.

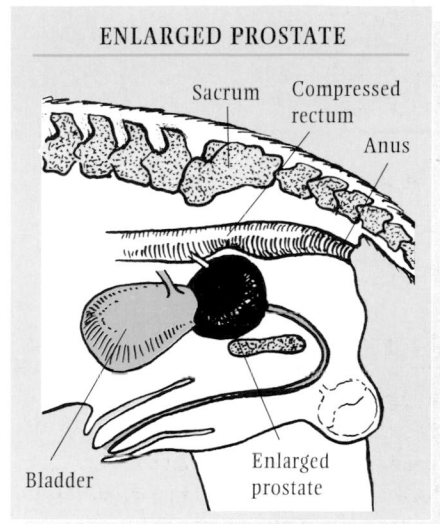

**ENLARGED PROSTATE**

Sacrum

Compressed rectum

Anus

Bladder

Enlarged prostate

- **Prostate disease**
This is common in the older un neutered Retriever. Usually a benign enlargement occurs where the prostate slowly increases in size. Hormone treatment or castration helps.
- **Infection of the penis and sheath**
Balanitis is an increase and discolouration occurs in the discharge from the sheath, and the dog licks his penis more frequently.
- **Paraphimosis**
Prolapse of the penis (see page 140).
- **Castration**
This is of value in the treatment of some behavioural problems. Excessive sexual activity, such as mounting cushions or other dogs, and territorial urination may be eliminated by castration, as may certain types of aggression and the desire to escape and wander.

## The bitch

- **Pyometra**
This is a common and serious disease of the older bitch although bitches which have had

## THE REPRODUCTIVE SYSTEM

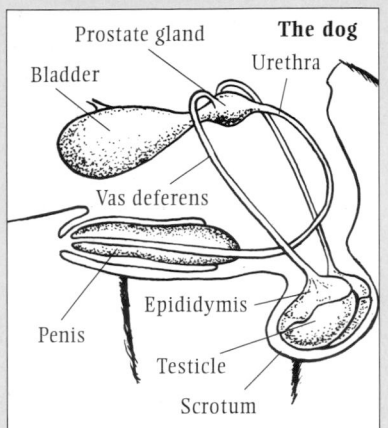

The dog

Prostate gland
Urethra
Bladder
Vas deferens
Epididymis
Penis
Testicle
Scrotum

Sperm and testosterone are produced in the male dog's testicles. Sperm pass into the epididymis for storage, thence via the vas deferens during mating.

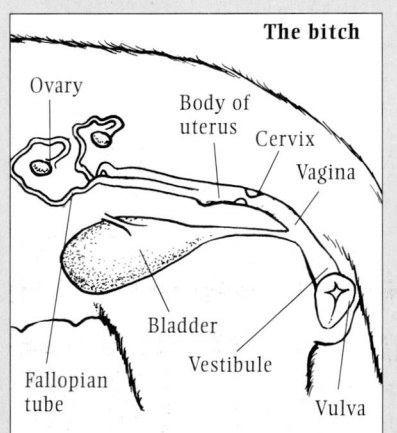

The bitch

Ovary
Body of uterus
Cervix
Vagina
Bladder
Vestibule
Fallopian tube
Vulva

Eggs are produced in the ovaries and enter the uterus through the fallopian tubes. During the heat period, they can be fertilized by sperm.

puppies seem less likely to develop it. The treatment is usually an ovariohysterectomy.

■ **Mastitis**

This is an infection of the mammary glands and occurs usually in lactating bitches. The affected glands become swollen, hard, and painful.

■ **Mammary tumours**

These are common in the older entire bitch. Most mammary tumours are benign, but where malignant, they can grow rapidly and spread to other organs. Early surgical removal of any lump is advisable because of the danger of malignancy.

■ **False or pseudo-pregnancy**

This occurs in most bitches about eight to twelve weeks after oestrus at the stage when the bitch would be lactating had she been pregnant. The signs vary and include poor appetite, lethargy, milk production, nest building, aggressiveness and attachment to a substitute puppy which is often a squeaky toy. Once a bitch has had a false pregnancy, she is likely to have one after each heat period.

■ **Treatment,** if needed, is by hormones, and prevention is by a hormone injection, or tablets, or an ovariohysterectomy.

■ **Eclampsia**

This is a very serious condition of the recently whelped bitch and can be fatal. The time of onset varies but it is usually seen when the pups are about three weeks old and making maximum demands on her. Her blood calcium level becomes too low due to the demands of the pups on her milk and she begins to show nervous symptoms. Initially she starts to twitch or shiver and appears unsteady, but this rapidly progresses to staggering, then convulsions. The vet must be contacted immediately as an injection of calcium is essential to save the life of the bitch.

# Birth control

## ■ Hormone therapy

Several preparations, injections and tablets are available to prevent or postpone the bitch's heat period.

## ■ Spaying (ovariohysterectomy)

This is an operation to remove the uterus and ovaries, usually performed when the bitch is not on heat. It is the better long-term alternative.

## NERVOUS SYSTEM DISEASES

The nervous system consists of two parts.

### 1 The central nervous system (CNS)

The brain and the spinal cord which runs in the vertebral column.

### 2 The peripheral nervous system

All the nerves which connect the CNS to the organs of the body.

## ■ Canine distemper virus

(See Infectious Diseases, page 108)

## ■ Vestibular syndrome

This is a fairly common condition of the older dog, and affects that part of the brain which controls balance. There is a sudden head tilt to the affected side, often flicking movements of the eyes called nystagmus, and the dog may fall or circle to that side. Many dogs will recover slowly but the condition may recur.

## ■ Slugbait (Metaldehyde) poisoning

The dog appears 'drunk', uncoordinated, and may have convulsions. There is no specific treatment, but sedation will often lead to recovery in a large dog like the Retriever.

## ■ Epilepsy

This seems particularly common in the Golden Retriever and is a nervous disorder causing fits. The dog has a sudden, unexpected fit or convulsion, which lasts for about two minutes. Recovery is fairly quick, although the dog may be dull and look confused for a few hours. Treatment is usually necessary and successful as far as control of epilepsy is concerned.

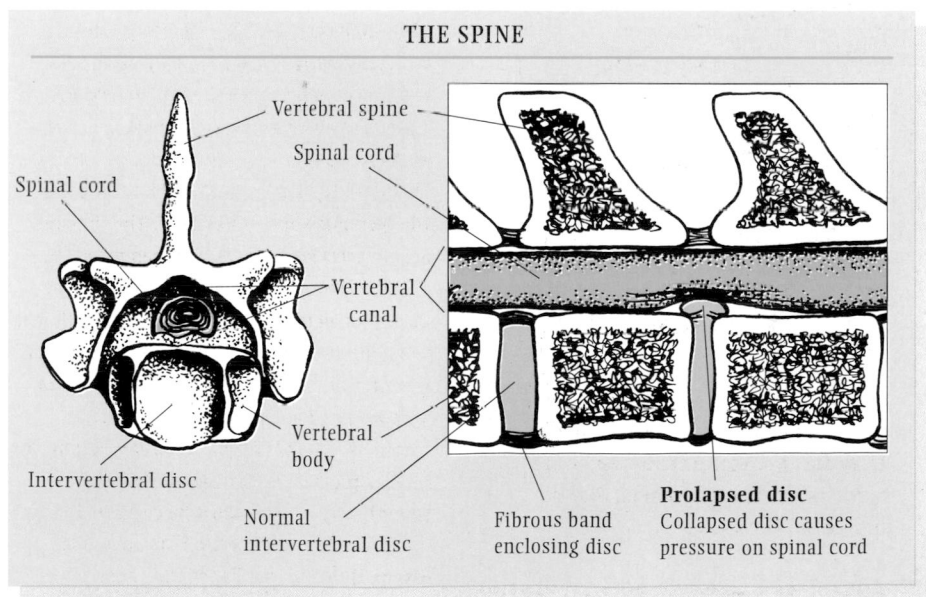

## THE SPINE

Vertebral spine

Spinal cord

Spinal cord

Vertebral canal

Intervertebral disc

Vertebral body

Normal intervertebral disc

Fibrous band enclosing disc

**Prolapsed disc**
Collapsed disc causes pressure on spinal cord

## BONE, MUSCLE AND JOINT DISEASES

X-rays are necessary to confirm any diagnosis involving bone.

### Bone infection (osteomyelitis)

This usually occurs after an injury such as a bite, or where a broken bone protrudes through the skin. Signs are pain, heat and swelling over the site, and if a limb bone is affected, there can be severe lameness.

### ■ Fractures

Any break or crack in a bone is called a fracture. When a vet repairs a fracture, his aim is to replace the fractured ends of bone into their normal position and then to immobilize the bone for four to six weeks. Depending on the bone, and type of fracture, there are several methods available cage rest, external casts, or surgery to perform internal fixation, by, for example, plating or pinning.

### ■ Bone tumours

These are not common, except in the giant breeds, but they are known to occur in the Retriever. The most common sites are the radius, humerus, and femur. Bone tumours are very painful, and they tend to be malignant and spread to other parts of the body early in the course of the disease. Amputation of the limb will remove the primary tumour but as it may have already spread to other areas, it is often not feasible. Radiotherapy and chemotherapy are not normally successful.

### ■ Sprains

A sprain is an inflammation of over-stretched joint ligaments. The joint is hot, swollen and painful, and the dog is lame.

### ■ Cruciate ligament rupture

When these rupture, as a result of a severe sprain, the stifle or knee joint is destabilized and the dog becomes instantly and severely lame on that leg. This occurs in middle-aged

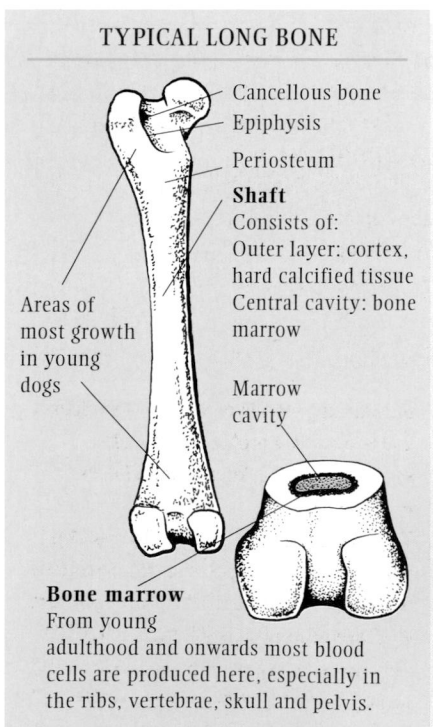

### TYPICAL LONG BONE

Cancellous bone
Epiphysis
Periosteum
**Shaft**
Consists of:
Outer layer: cortex, hard calcified tissue
Central cavity: bone marrow

Areas of most growth in young dogs

Marrow cavity

**Bone marrow**
From young adulthood and onwards most blood cells are produced here, especially in the ribs, vertebrae, skull and pelvis.

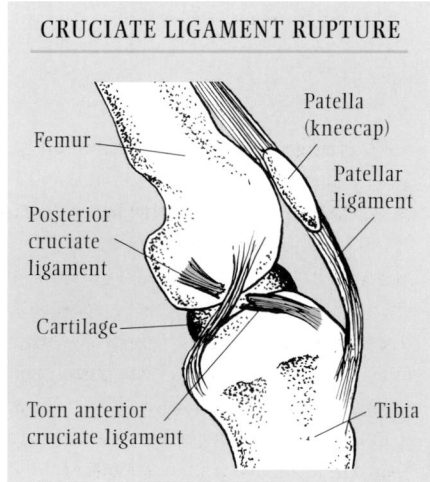

### CRUCIATE LIGAMENT RUPTURE

Patella (kneecap)
Femur
Patellar ligament
Posterior cruciate ligament
Cartilage
Torn anterior cruciate ligament
Tibia

## TYPES OF FRACTURES

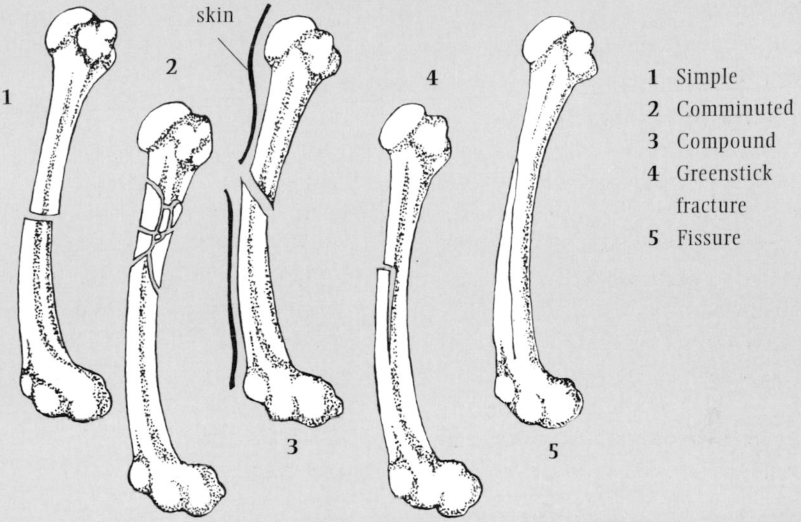

skin

1 Simple
2 Comminuted
3 Compound
4 Greenstick fracture
5 Fissure

Most broken bones are the result of accidents, especially road traffic ones when dogs are run over by cars. However, puppies are also susceptible to fractures if they are trodden on accidentally or dropped.

Five types of fracture are shown above:

■ **Simple fracture:** the bone is broken into two pieces at one site

■ **Comminuted fracture:** the bone is broken into several pieces

■ **Compound fracture:** the skin is penetrated by a broken bone end

■ **Greenstick fracture:** the break is incomplete with part of the bone remaining intact

■ **Fissure:** the bone is cracked

and overweight Retrievers. Surgical repair is usually necessary.

■ **Arthritis or degenerative joint disease**
This is common in the Retriever, where it invariably follows hip dysplasia, or OCD in an affected joint (see Special Diseases, page 106). It results in thickening of the joint capsule, formation of abnormal new bone around the edges of the joint and, sometimes, wearing of the joint cartilage. The joint becomes enlarged and painful, and has a reduced range of movement. It tends to occur in the older dog and is usually a problem of the hips, shoulders, stifles (knees), and elbows.

■ **Spondylitis**
This is arthritis of the spine. This is also common in the older Retriever and causes weakness and stiffness of the hindquarters.

■ **Osteochondritis dissicans (OCD)**
This disease occurs in the shoulder and other joints but is uncommon in the Golden, Flat Coated and Curly Coated Retrievers,

## THE SKELETON

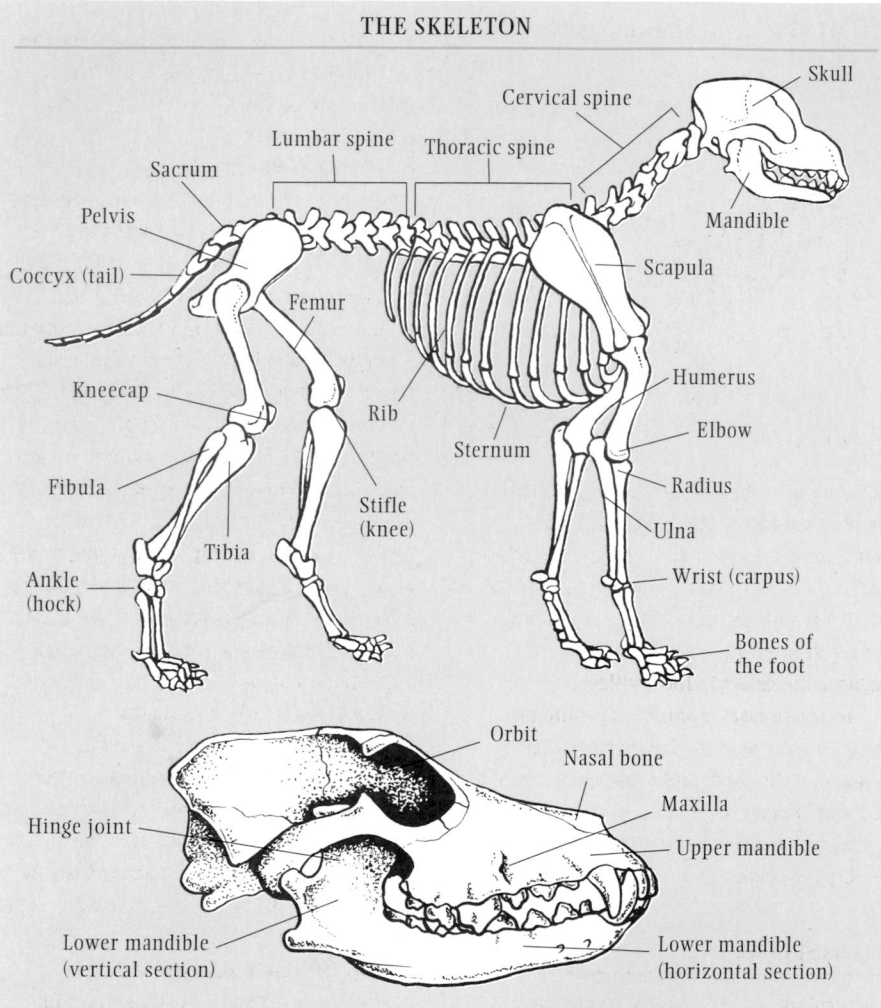

Skull

Cervical spine

Lumbar spine     Thoracic spine

Sacrum

Mandible

Pelvis

Coccyx (tail)

Scapula

Femur

Humerus

Kneecap

Rib

Elbow

Sternum

Fibula

Radius

Stifle
(knee)

Ulna

Tibia

Ankle
(hock)

Wrist (carpus)

Bones of
the foot

Orbit       Nasal bone

Hinge joint

Maxilla

Upper mandible

Lower mandible
(vertical section)

Lower mandible
(horizontal section)

The skeleton is the framework for the body. All the dog's ligaments, muscles and tendons are attached to the bones, 319 of them in total. By a process called ossification, cartilage template is calcified to produce bone. Bones are living tissue and they respond to the stresses and strains placed upon them. To build and keep healthy bones, dogs need a nutritionally balanced diet which contains an adequate supply of calcium, vitamin D and phosphorus.

## TYPICAL NORMAL JOINT

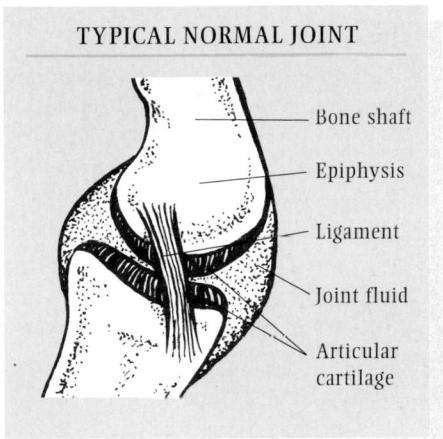

Bone shaft

Epiphysis

Ligament

Joint fluid

Articular cartilage

compared with the Labrador Retriever. The dog becomes lame between six and nine months of age due to a piece of joint cartilage breaking away from the underlying bone. Usually more than one joint is affected but to varying degrees. An X-ray is necessary to diagnose the defect in the cartilage.

In severe cases, a surgical operation is necessary to remove the loose or detached fragment. If the condition is untreated the joint may become arthritic, or the piece of cartilage may move around in the joint, causing great pain.

## Hip dysplasia (IID)

Hip dysplasia is the commonest, and most serious of the developmental abnormalities of the Retriever. In a normal dog the hip is a 'ball and socket' joint and allows a wide range of movement. The rounded end at the top of the femur, the femoral head, fits tightly into the acetabulum in the pelvis, a deep, cup-shaped socket. Hip dysplasia is the development instead of a shallow acetabulum, an irregular, distorted head of the femur, and

slackness of the joint ligaments. Excessive movement can and does occur between the femur and the pelvis, and this leads to a malfunctioning, painful joint which will gradually become arthritic.

- **Causes of hip dysplasia**

It is known to be inherited but there are other factors involved, such as poor nutrition, too much exercise, or even being overweight during the rapid growth phase of the young dog.

- **Early signs of hip dysplasia in puppies**

A puppy developing severe hip dysplasia may have great difficulty walking, and particularly standing up from a sitting position which he may find painful and cry out. He may appear to sway when running, or characteristically use both hind legs together in a bunny hop. These signs may be present as young as five months old. Mildly affected puppies may show no signs at all at this stage, but at about eight years of age begin to develop arthritis.

- **Confirming hip dysplasia**

Your vet will suspect hip dysplasia in a Retriever with the above symptoms at the right age. Confirmation is by manipulation of the suspect joint and by an X-ray. This should be carried out under general anaesthetic for safety reasons for the operator, and for correct positioning of the dog.

- **Hip dysplasia scheme**

All Retrievers, of both sexes, intended for breeding should be X-rayed at not less than one year of age. The British Veterinary Association and the Kennel Club have for many years run a joint scheme (the BVA/KC hip dysplasia scheme) based on hip scoring, and the vet submits the X-ray, bearing the KC registration number of the dog, to the scheme. Each hip is scored from 0 to 54, making a total of 108 maximum between the two hips.

The lower the score the better, and 0:0 is the best score possible.

So far over 15,300 X-rays have been submitted for scrutiny and the average combined score for the Golden Retriever is 20, for the Flat Coated, 9 (2276), and for the Curly Coated, 11 (117). No-one should breed from a dog or bitch with a higher hip score than the average for the breed if HD is ever to be reduced or eliminated from that breed. Anyone buying a puppy should ensure both parents have been X-rayed, scored, and achieved a low score. This is not, of course, an absolute guarantee that the puppy will not develop hip dysplasia, but it should considerably reduce the chances.

■ **Treatment** If the hip dysplasia is diagnosed at an early stage, and is mild, a combination of anabolic steroids, restricted exercise, and a slightly underweight dog during the growth phase will often lead to a sound adult dog. He may, however, only be able to indulge in a limited amount of exercise during his life. Too much at this stage may lead to arthritis later. In more severe cases, one of several available surgical techniques will be needed, but the dog will never be as agile as an unaffected dog.

## HIP DYSPLASIA

### NORMAL HIP JOINT

Head of femur
Neck
Acetabulum
Pelvis
Femur

This normal hip would score 0 on the BVA/KC hip dysplasia scheme.

### HIP DYSPLASIA

Enlarged joint space
Shallow socket
Flattened head
Femur
Thickened neck

This abnormal hip would score approximately 26 on the BVA/KC hip dysplasia scheme giving a total score of 52 if the other hip was similarly deformed.

# CHAPTER TEN

# FIRST AID, ACCIDENTS AND EMERGENCIES

First aid is the emergency care given to a dog suffering injury or illness of sudden onset.

## AIMS OF FIRST AID

**1 Keep the dog alive.**
**2 Prevent unnecessary suffering.**
**3 Prevent further injury.**

## RULES OF FIRST AID

**Keep calm.** If you panic you will be unable to help effectively.

**Contact a vet as soon as possible.** Advice given over the telephone may be life-saving.

**Avoid injury to yourself.** A distressed or injured animal may bite so use a muzzle if necessary (see muzzling, page 140).

**Control haemorrhage.** Excessive blood loss can lead to severe shock and death (see haemorrhage, page 133).

**Maintain an airway.** Failure to breathe or obtain adequate oxygen can lead to brain damage or loss of life within five minutes (see airway obstruction and artificial respiration, page 131).

## COMMON ACCIDENTS AND EMERGENCIES

The following common accidents and emergencies all require first aid action. In an emergency, your priorities are to keep the dog alive and comfortable until he can be examined by a vet. In many cases, there is effective action that you can take immediately to help preserve your dog's health and life.

SHOCK AND ROAD ACCIDENTS

*(vertical left margin)* SHOCK AND ROAD ACCIDENTS

## SHOCK

This is a serious clinical syndrome which can cause death. Shock can follow road accidents, severe burns, electrocution, extremes of heat and cold, heart failure, poisoning, severe fluid loss, reactions to drugs, insect stings or snake bite.

### SIGNS OF SHOCK
- Weakness or collapse
- Pale gums
- Cold extremities, e.g. feet and ears
- Weak pulse and rapid heart
- Rapid, shallow breathing

### RECOMMENDED ACTION

**1**
Act immediately. Give cardiac massage (see page 132) and/or artificial respiration (see page 131) if necessary, after checking for a clear airway.

**2**
Keep the dog flat and warm. Control external haemorrhage ( page 133).

**3**
Veterinary treatment is essential thereafter.

## ROAD ACCIDENTS

Injuries resulting from a fast-moving vehicle colliding with an animal can be very serious. Road accidents may result in:
- Death
- Head injuries
- Spinal damage
- Internal haemorrhage, bruising and rupture of major organs, e.g. liver, spleen, kidneys
- Fractured ribs and lung damage, possibly resulting in haemothorax (blood in the chest cavity) or pneumothorax (air in the chest cavity)
- Fractured limbs with or without nerve damage
- External haemorrhage, wounds, tears and bruising

### RECOMMENDED ACTION

**1**
Assess the situation and move the dog to a safe position. Use a blanket to transport him and keep him flat.

**2**
Check for signs of life: feel for a heart beat (see cardiac massage, page 132), and watch for the rise and fall of the chest wall.

**3**
If the dog is breathing, treat as for shock (see above). If he is not breathing but there is a heart beat, give artificial respiration, after checking for airway obstruction. Consider the use of a muzzle (see muzzling, page 140).

**4**
Control external haemorrhage (see haemorrhage, page 133).

**5**
Keep the dog warm and flat at all times, and seek veterinary help.

# AIRWAY OBSTRUCTION

■ **FOREIGN BODY IN THE THROAT,** e.g. a ball.

■ **FOLLOWING A ROAD ACCIDENT**, or convulsion, blood, saliva or vomit in the throat may obstruct breathing.

## RECOMMENDED ACTION

### 1

This is an acute emergency. Do not try to pull out the object. Push it upwards and forwards from behind the throat so that it moves from its position where it is obstructing the larynx, into the mouth.

### 2

The dog should now be able to breathe. Remove the object from his mouth.

## RECOMMENDED ACTION

### 1

Pull the tongue forwards and clear any obstruction with your fingers.

### 2

Then, with the dog on his side, extend the head and neck forwards to maintain a clear airway.

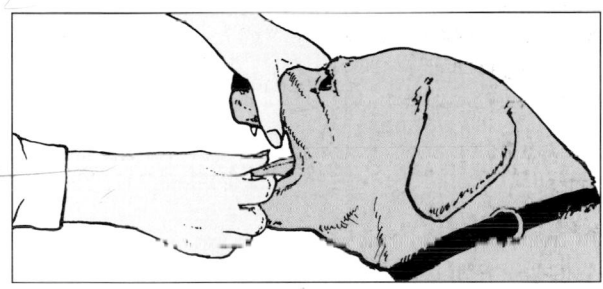

# DROWNING

## RECOMMENDED ACTION

### 1

Out of the water, remove collar and place dog on his side with his head lower than his body.

### 2

With hands, apply firm downward pressure on chest at five-second intervals.

# ARTIFICIAL RESPIRATION

The method for helping a dog which has a clear airway but cannot breathe.

## RECOMMENDED ACTION

Use mouth-to-mouth resuscitation by cupping your hands over his nose and mouth and blowing into his nostrils every five seconds.

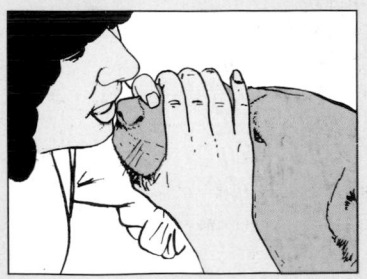

## CARDIAC MASSAGE

This is required if your dog's heart fails.

**RECOMMENDED ACTION**

With the dog lying on his right side, feel for a heart beat with your fingers on the chest wall behind the dog's elbows on his left side.

Listen for a heart beat

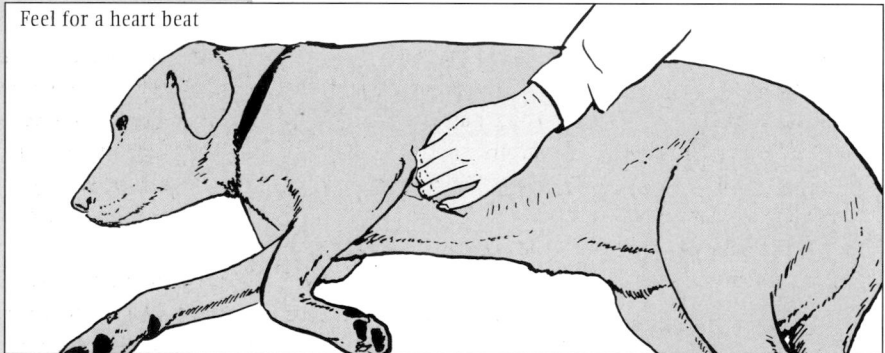

Feel for a heart beat

**2**

If you feel nothing, squeeze rhythmically with your palms, placing one hand on top of the other, as shown, at two-second intervals, pressing down hard.

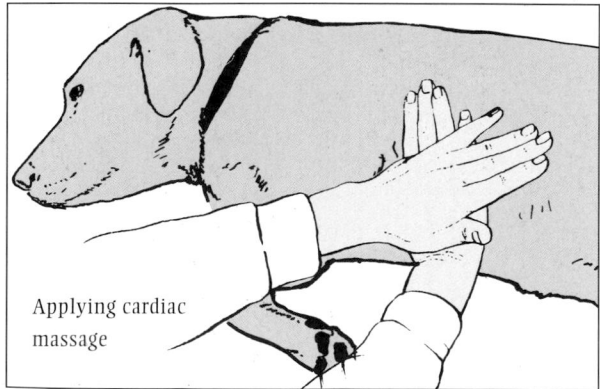

Applying cardiac massage

# HAEMORRHAGE

Severe haemorrhage must be controlled, as it leads to a precipitous fall in blood pressure and the onset of shock. Haemorrhage is likely to result from deep surface wounds, or internal injuries, e.g. following a road accident.

■ **FOR SURFACE WOUNDS**

### RECOMMENDED ACTION

Locate the bleeding point and apply pressure either with:
■ **Your thumb** or
■ **A pressure bandage** (preferred method) or
■ **A tourniquet**

**1** **Pressure bandage**
Use a pad of gauze, cotton wool or cloth against the wound and tightly bandage around it. In the

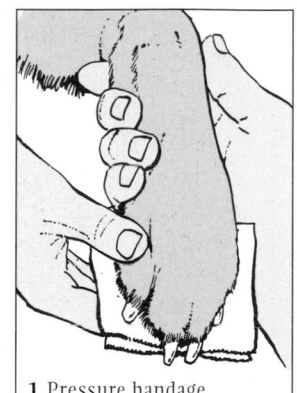

1 Pressure bandage

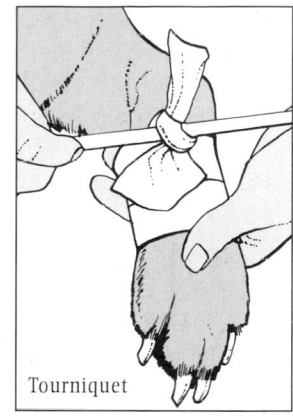

Tourniquet

absence of a proper dressing, use a clean handkerchief or scarf.

**2** If the bleeding continues, apply another dressing on top of the first.

**1** **Tourniquet** (on limbs and tail)
Tie a narrow piece of cloth, a neck tie or dog lead tightly

around the limb, nearer to the body than the wound itself.

**2** Using a pencil or stick within the knot, twist until it becomes tight enough to stop the blood flow.

**3** **Important**: you must seek veterinary assistance as soon as possible.

**Note: Tourniquets should be applied for no longer than fifteen minutes at a time, or tissue death may result.**

■ **FOR INTERNAL BLEEDING**

### RECOMMENDED ACTION

**1** You should keep the animal quiet and warm, and minimize any movement.

**2** **Important**: you must seek veterinary assistance as soon as possible.

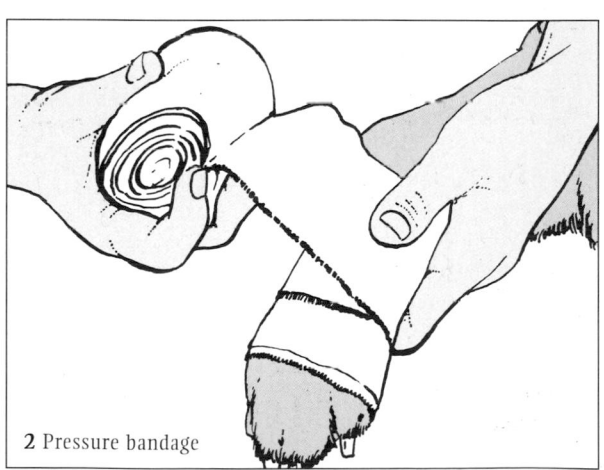

2 Pressure bandage

# WOUNDS

These may result from road accidents, dog fights, sharp stones or glass, etc. Deep wounds may cause serious bleeding, bone or nerve damage.

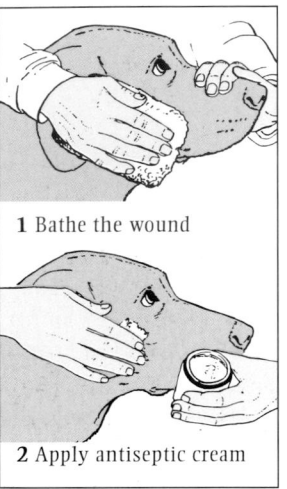

1 Bathe the wound

2 Apply antiseptic cream

## RECOMMENDED ACTION

**1** Deal with external bleeding (see haemorrhage, page 133) and keep the dog quiet before seeking veterinary attention.

**2** Cut feet or pads should be bandaged to prevent further blood loss.

**3** Minor cuts, abrasions and bruising should be bathed with warm salt solution (one 5ml teaspoonful per 550ml (1 pint) of water). They should be protected from further injury or contamination. Apply some antiseptic cream, if necessary.

**4** If in doubt, ask your vet in case a wound needs suturing or antibiotic therapy is needed, particularly if caused by fighting. Even minor cuts and punctures can be complicated by the presence of a foreign body.

# FRACTURES

Broken bones, especially in the legs, often result from road accidents. Be careful when lifting and transporting the affected dog.

◂ **LEG FRACTURES**

### RECOMMENDED ACTION

**1** Broken lower leg bones can sometimes be straightened gently, bandaged and taped or tied with string to a make-shift splint, e.g. a piece of wood or rolled-up newspaper or cardboard.

**2** Otherwise, support the leg to prevent any movement. Take the dog to the vet immediately.

■ **OTHER FRACTURES**
These may be more difficult to diagnose. If you suspect a fracture, transport your dog very gently and with great care, and get him to the vet.

# OTHER ACCIDENTS AND EMERGENCIES

## COLLAPSE

This may be accompanied by loss of consciousness, but not in every case.

**POSSIBLE CAUSES**
- Head trauma, e.g. following a road accident
- Heart failure
- Stroke
- Hyperthermia (heat-stroke)
- Hypothermia (cold)
- Hypocalcaemia (low calcium)
- Shock
- Spinal fractures
- Asphyxia (interference with breathing)
- Electrocution
- Poisoning

**Note:** you should refer to the relevant section for further details of these problems.

### RECOMMENDED ACTION

**1** The collapsed animal must be moved with care to avoid further damage.

**2** Gently slide him on his side onto a blanket or coat.

**3** Check he is breathing, and then keep him quiet and warm until you obtain professional help.

**4** If he is not breathing, administer artificial respiration immediately, after checking for a clear airway (see page 131).

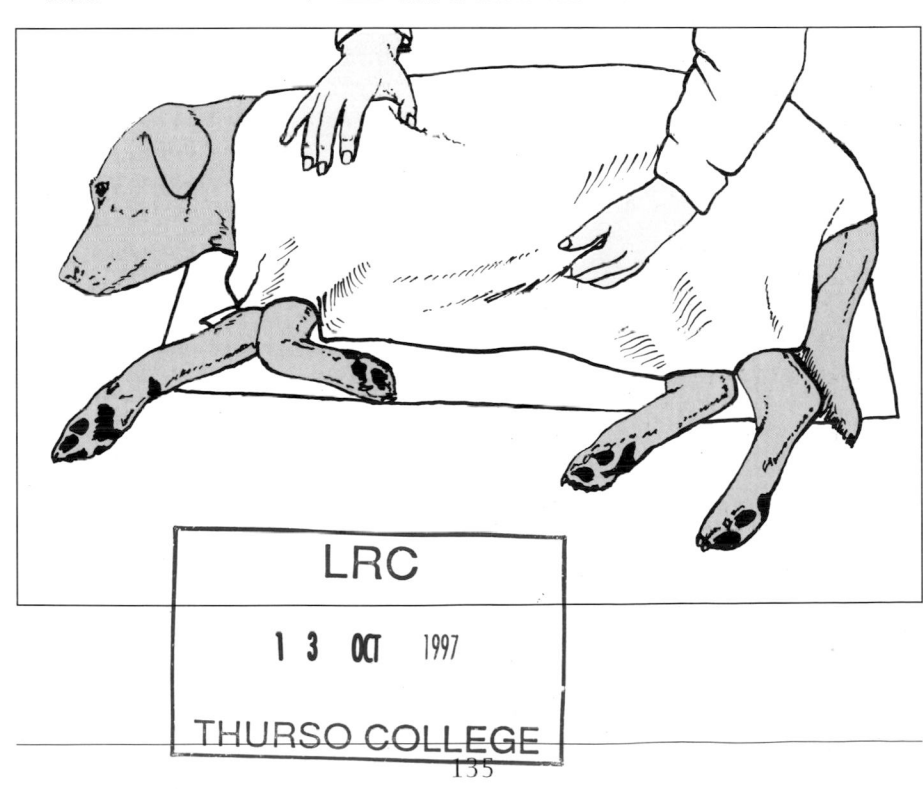

# CONVULSIONS (FITS OR SEIZURES)

These are very alarming to dog owners. Uncontrolled spasms, 'paddling' of legs, loss of consciousness, sometimes salivation and involuntary urination or defaecation occur. Most convulsions only last a few minutes, but the dog is often confused and dazed afterwards.

**POSSIBLE CAUSES**
- Poisoning
- Head injuries
- Brain tumours
- Liver and kidney disease
- Meningitis
- Epilepsy
- Low blood glucose, e.g. in diabetes, or low blood calcium, e.g. in eclampsia

## RECOMMENDED ACTION

**1** Unless he is in a dangerous situation, do not attempt to hold the dog, but protect him from damaging himself.

**2** Do not give your Retriever anything by mouth.

**3** Try to keep him quiet, cool and in a darkened room until he sees the vet.

**4** If you have to move your Retriever, you should cover him with a blanket first.

# HEART FAILURE

This is not common in the Retriever. Affected dogs faint, usually during exercise, and lose consciousness. The mucous membranes appear pale or slightly blue.

## RECOMMENDED ACTION

**1** Cover the dog in a blanket, lie him on his side.

**2** Massage his chest behind the elbows (see cardiac massage, page 132).

**3** When he recovers, take him straight to the vet.

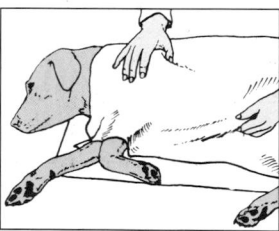

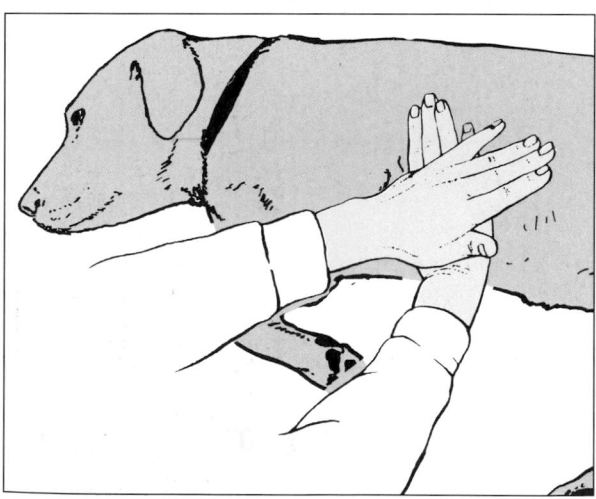

1 An affected dog should be covered with a blanket and laid on his side.
2 Apply cardiac massage, pressing down firmly at two-second intervals.

# HEAT-STROKE

This occurs in hot weather, especially when dogs have been left in cars. With his heavy coat, the Retriever is likely to feel the heat. Affected animals are extremely distressed, panting and possibly collapsed. They can die rapidly. A heat-stroke case should be treated as an acute emergency.

### RECOMMENDED ACTION

**1** Either place the dog in a cold bath or run cold water over his body until his temperature is in the normal range.

**2** Offer water with added salt (one 5ml teaspoonful per half litre/1 pint water).

**3** Treatment for shock may be necessary (see page 130).

# ELECTROCUTION

This is most likely to occur in a bored puppy who chews through a cable. Electrocution may kill him outright or lead to delayed shock.

■ **DO NOT TOUCH HIM BEFORE YOU SWITCH OFF THE ELECTRICITY SOURCE.**

### RECOMMENDED ACTION

**1** If he is not breathing, begin artificial respiration immediately (see page 131) and keep him warm.

**2** Contact your vet; if he survives he will need treatment for shock (see page 130).

# BURNS AND SCALDS

**POSSIBLE CAUSES**
■ Spilled hot drinks, boiling water or fat.
■ Friction, chemical and electrical burns.

### RECOMMENDED ACTION

**1** Immediately apply running cold water and, thereafter, cold compresses, ice packs or packets of frozen peas to the affected area.

**2** Veterinary attention is essential in most cases.

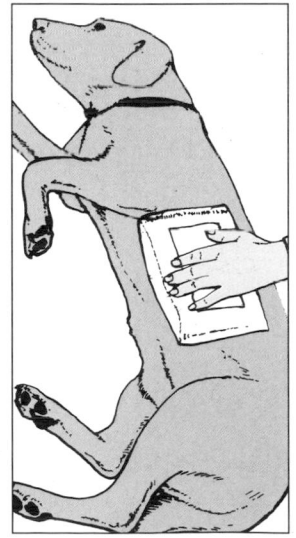

# SNAKE BITE

This is due to the adder in Great Britain. Signs are pain accompanied by a soft swelling around two puncture wounds, usually on either the head, neck or limbs. Trembling, collapse, shock and even death can ensue.

### RECOMMENDED ACTION

**1** Do not let the dog walk; carry him to the car.

**2** Keep him warm, and take him immediately to the vet.

Other accidents and emergencies

## FOREIGN BODIES

■ **IN THE MOUTH**
Sticks or bones wedged between the teeth cause frantic pawing at the mouth and salivation.

### RECOMMENDED ACTION

Remove the foreign body with your fingers or pliers. Use a wooden block placed between the dog's canine teeth if possible to aid the safety of this procedure. Some objects have to be removed under general anaesthesia.
**Note:** a ball in the throat is dealt with in airway obstruction (see page 131), and is a critical emergency.

■ **FISH HOOKS**
Never try to pull these out, wherever they are.

### RECOMMENDED ACTION

Push the fish hook through the skin, cut the line end off with pliers, and then pull it out.

■ **IN THE FOOT**
Glass, thorns or splinters can penetrate the pads or soft skin, causing pain, and infection if neglected.

### RECOMMENDED ACTION

Soak the foot in warm salt water and then use a sharp

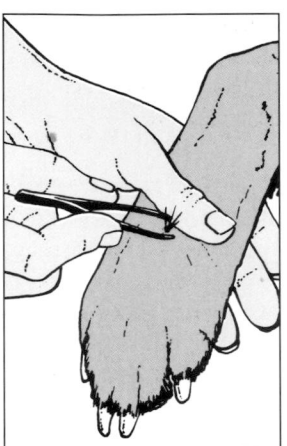

sterilized needle or pair of tweezers to extract the foreign body. If this is not possible, take your dog to the vet who will remove it under local or general anaesthetic if necessary.

■ **IN THE EAR**
The hairy ears of a Retriever can attract little spiky grass seeds, which are a real nuisance to dogs. If one finds its way into an ear, it can produce sudden severe distress and violent head shaking.

### RECOMMENDED ACTION

If you can see the seed, gently but firmly pull it out with tweezers, and check it is intact. If you cannot see it, or feel you may have left some in, call the vet immediately.

## NOSE BLEEDS

These may be caused by trauma or violent sneezing, but are also related in some cases to ulceration of the lining of the nasal cavity.

### RECOMMENDED ACTION

**1** Keep the dog quiet and use ice packs on the nose.

**2** Contact your vet if the bleeding persists.

## EYEBALL PROLAPSE

This is not a common problem in Retrievers, but it may arise from head trauma, e.g. following a dog fight. The eye is forced out of its socket and sight is lost unless it is replaced within fifteen minutes.

### RECOMMENDED ACTION

**1** Speed is essential. One person should pull the eyelids apart while the other gently presses the eyeball back into its socket, using moist sterile gauze or cloth.

**2** If this is impossible, cover the eye with moist sterile gauze and take the dog to your vet immediately.

## GASTRIC DILATION

This is an emergency and cannot be treated at home. The stomach distends with gas and froth which the dog cannot easily eliminate. In some cases, the stomach then rotates and a torsion occurs, so the gases cannot escape at all and the stomach rapidly fills the abdomen.

This causes pain, respiratory distress and circulatory failure. Life-threatening shock follows.

### PREVENTIVE ACTION

**1** Avoid the problem by not exercising your Retriever vigorously for two hours after a full meal.

**2** If your dog is becoming bloated and has difficulty breathing, he is unlikely to survive unless he has veterinary attention within half an hour of the onset of symptoms, so get your Retriever to the vet immediately.

## POISONING

Dogs can be poisoned by pesticides, herbicides, poisonous plants, paints, antifreeze or an overdose of drugs (animal or human).

■ If poisoning is suspected, first try to determine the agent involved, and find out if it is corrosive or not. This may be indicated on the container, but may also be evident from the blistering of the lips, gums and tongue, and increased salivation.

### RECOMMENDED ACTION

■ **CORROSIVE POISONS**

**1** Wash the inside of the dog's mouth.

**2** Give him milk and bread to protect the gut against the effects of the corrosive.

**3** Seek veterinary help.

■ **OTHER POISONS**

**1** If the dog is conscious, make him vomit within half an hour of taking the poison.

**2** A crystal of washing soda or a few 15ml tablespoonfuls of strong salt solution can be given carefully by mouth.

**3** Retain a sample of vomit to aid identification of the poison, or take the poison container with you to show the vet. There may be a specific antidote, and any information can help in treatment.

## STINGS

Bee and wasp stings often occur around the head, front limbs or mouth. The dog usually shows sudden pain and paws at, or licks, the stung area. A soft, painful swelling appears; sometimes the dog seems unwell or lethargic. Stings in the mouth and throat can be distressing and dangerous.

### RECOMMENDED ACTION

**1** Withdraw the sting (bees).

**2** Then you can bathe the area in:

■ Vinegar for wasps

■ Bicarbonate for bees

**3** An antihistamine injection may be needed.

OTHER ACCIDENTS AND EMERGENCIES

# BREEDING

■ **ECLAMPSIA**

This is a very serious condition of the recently whelped bitch and can be fatal. Initially she starts to twitch and appears unsteady. This progresses to staggering, then convulsions.

## RECOMMENDED ACTION

Contact the vet immediately as an injection of calcium is essential to save her life. Keep her warm and, if you have any, administer calcium colloidal suspension or a calcium tablet in the meantime.

■ **PARAPHIMOSIS**

This problem may occur after mating, in the male. The engorged penis is unable to retract into the sheath.

## RECOMMENDED ACTION

The exposed penis should be bathed in cool, sterile water to reduce its size. Lubricate with petroleum jelly or soap to pull the sheath forward. If correction is impossible, ring the vet.

# MUZZLING

This will allow a nervous, distressed or injured dog to be examined safely, without the risk of being bitten. A tape or bandage is secured around the muzzle as illustrated. However, a muzzle should not be applied in the following circumstances:

■ Airway obstruction

■ Loss of consciousness

■ Compromised breathing or severe chest injury

1 Tie a knot in the bandage.

2 Wrap around the dog's muzzle with the knot under the lower jaw and tie on top of the muzzle.

3 Cross the ends under the jaw and tie firmly behind the dog's head.

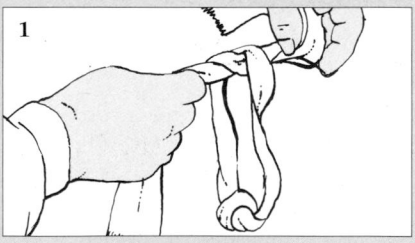

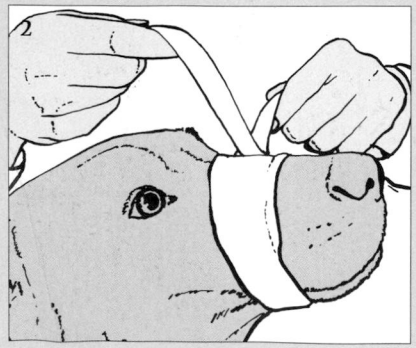

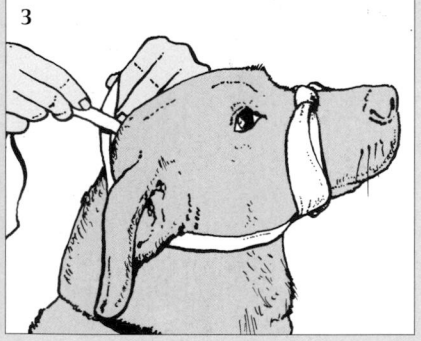

# GLOSSARY

**Angulation**
The angles created by bones meeting at a joint.

**Breed standard**
The description laid down by the Kennel Club of the perfect breed specimen.

**Brood bitch**
A female dog which is used for breeding.

**Carpals**
These are the wrist bones.

**Croup**
This is the dog's rump: the front of the pelvis to the start of the tail.

**Dam**
The mother of puppies.

**Dew claw**
A fifth toe above the ground on the inside of the legs.

**Elbow**
The joint at the top of the forearm below the upper arm.

**Flank**
The area between the last rib and hip on the side of the body.

**Furnishings**
The long hair on the head, legs, thighs, back of buttocks or tail.

**Gait**
How a dog moves at different speeds.

**Guard hairs**
Long hairs that grow through the undercoat.

**Muzzle**
The foreface, or front of the head.

**Occiput**
The back upper part of the skull.

**Oestrus**
The periods when a bitch is 'on heat' or 'in season' and responsive to mating.

**Pastern**
Between the wrist (carpus) and the digits of the forelegs.

**Scissor bite**
Strong jaws with upper teeth overlapping lower ones.

**Stifle**
The hind leg joint, or 'knee'.

**Undercoat**
A dense, short coat hidden below the top-coat.

**Whelping**
The act of giving birth.

**Whelps**
Puppies that have not been weaned.

**Whiskers**
Long hairs on the jaw and muzzle.

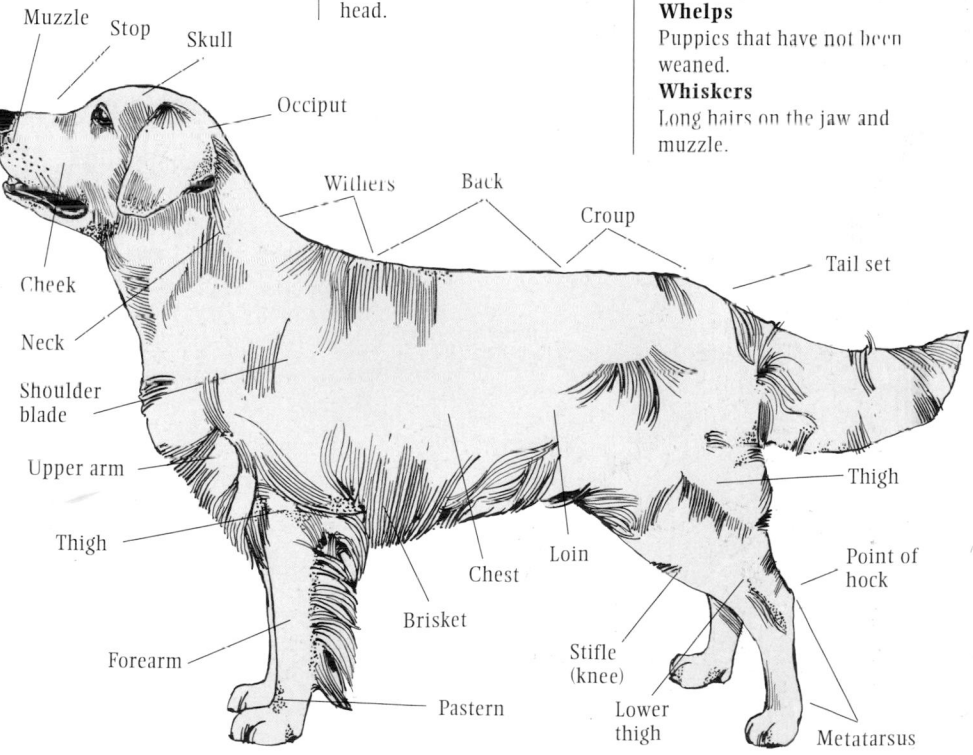

Muzzle　Stop　Skull　Occiput　Withers　Back　Croup　Tail set　Cheek　Neck　Shoulder blade　Upper arm　Thigh　Forearm　Brisket　Chest　Pastern　Loin　Stifle (knee)　Lower thigh　Thigh　Point of hock　Metatarsus

# INDEX

# USEFUL ADDRESSES

**Animal Aunts**
Wydnooch
45 Fairview Rd
Headley Down
Hampshire
GU38 8HQ
(Home sitters,
holidays)

**Animal Studies
Centre**
Waltham-on-the-Wolds
Melton Mowbray
Leics LE14 4RS
(Animal nutrition)

**Association of Pet
Behaviour
Counsellors**
257 Royal College St.
London
NW1 9LU

**British Veterinary
Association**
7 Mansfield Street
London W1M 0AT

**Dog Breeders
Insurance Co Ltd**
9 St Stephens Court
St Stephens Road

Bournemouth
BH2 6LG
(Books of cover notes
for dog breeders)

**Featherbed
Country Club**
High Wycombe
Bucks
(Luxury dog
accommodation)

**Guide Dogs for the
Blind Association**
Hillfield
Burghfield
Reading
RG7 3YG

**Hearing Dogs for
the Deaf**
The Training Centre
London Road
Lewknor
Oxon OX9 5RY

**Home Sitters**
Buckland Wharf
Buckland
Aylesbury
Bucks
HP22 5LO

**The Kennel Club**
1-5 Clarges Street
Piccadilly
London
W1Y 8AB
(Breed Standards,
Breed Club and Field
Trial contact
addresses, registration
forms, Good Citizen
training scheme)

**National Canine
Defence League**
1 & 2 Pratt Mews
London
NW1 0AD

**Pet Plan Insurance**
Westcross House
2 Westcross Way
Brentwood
Middlesex
TW8 9YP

**Pets As Therapy
(PAT Dogs)**
6 New Road
Ditton
Kent
ME20 6AD
(Information: how

friendly dogs can
join the hospital
visiting scheme)

**PRO Dogs National
Charity**
4 New Road,
Ditton
Kent
ME20 6AD
(Information: Better
British Breeders,
worming certificates
to provide with
puppies, how to cope
with grief on the loss
of a loved dog etc.)

**Royal Society for
the Prevention of
Cruelty to Animals**
RSPCA Headquarters
Causeway
Horsham
West Sussex
RH12 1HG

## SCAMPERS SCHOOL FOR DOGS

Scampers helps to train over 200 dogs and puppies every week, using kind, reward-based methods and behaviour therapy, in its unique indoor training facilities. Expert advice is given on all aspects of dog care, and there are puppy, beginners, intermediate and advanced classes. Scampers also run courses for other dog trainers and people interested in a career in dog training.
**Scampers Pet Products**
This specialist mail order service provides special products, including books, videos, toys, accessories and training equipment, for dog owners. It is based

at Scampers Petcare Superstore, which offers one of the largest ranges of dog accessories in the UK. For more information on Scampers School for Dogs, Scampers Petcare Superstore or Scampers Pet Products contact:
Scampers Petcare Superstore
Northfield Road
Soham
Nr. Ely
Cambs CB7 5UF
Tel: 01353 720431
Fax: 01353 624202